G000090812

The Spirit of Gin

History, Anecdotes, Trends and Cocktails

TEXTS BY Davide Terziotti and Vittorio d'Alberto

PHOTOGRAPHS BY Fabio Petroni

COCKTAILS BY Ekaterina Logvinova

Contents

العصب وسلح العضل و
القوى واوجاع الارحام ه

لوائى وهو الابهل
وهو الراس مرسمه انه وطور وهو صعار اجزا اسبه وروه والسرو وهو
اكبرشنا كامرعه من الابهل كرده الراحه وهى بلدهم والعوض اكبرمنها والطول
وهو الراس مرسه سطعل وروها
بلد النجوم والصف الاخر
ورقه سبه وورى الطرفا
وورى كلى النصعر ينفع
ينفع الفروح الخشنه وسكن
الاكله والاورام الحاده و
اذا ضمد به نقى سواد الجلد
وان ساحه الرى تعرض وصول
البدر وهس يشد كرشه
اللحم واذا شرب ابال الدم
واسقط الجنس واذا اخذل
وتدخره فعارلك وقد
يقع فى اخلاط ادرمان
مسيته وحاصه واخلاط دهر عصير الن ب

Introduction

The origin of many alcoholic beverages can be found in the therapeutic properties that were attributed to the herbs and spices used to make them. The parable of gin is similar to that of many other beverages and foods, made up of successes, failures and rebirths, including unexpected ones. Throughout all of its transformations, gin is inextricably linked to the plant from which it takes its name, the Juniper, cited in a myriad of medical preparations since antiquity. The Egyptians described the use of juniper to treat jaundice in the *Ebers Papyrus*. Pedanius Dioscorides, the great Greek physician who served in Emperor Nero's army, recommended adding juniper berries to wine to treat lung and bronchial diseases. In *Naturalis Historia*, Pliny the Elder sung their praises in various preparations, especially when mixed with wine. A work by the *Schola Medica Salernitana*, from around the year 1000, later translated into vernacular form and put beautifully into rhyme, says: *lo Ginepro ti da con poca spesa, sicurissime bacche: con le quali Medicine puoi fare di grand'impresa* ("The Juniper, at a reasonable cost, gives you very safe berries: with which Medicines can do great things"). Even at the height of the scientific revolution in the 1600s, juniper appears dozens of times in the manual *Universal Pharmacopoeia* by Nicolas Lémery, often mixed with spirits.

4 · *A picture of Savin juniper* (Juniperus sabina) *from the Arabian version of Pedanius Dioscorides'* De Materia Medica.

When we talk about gin and its history, we are talking about all of the stories about gin, about its centuries-long evolutionary journey, still in progress, linked to the function of this beverage, which differentiates itself from other similar spirits thanks to its characteristic of being a medium; an instrument. Despite centuries of evolution, the discovery of its use for medical purposes and its evolution through cocktails, gins "created" to be drunk "neat" have only appeared on the market in recent years.

Before we become absorbed in this fascinating story, there are a few things we'd like to point out. Firstly, although it played an important role in the history and evolution of gin as we know it today, its Dutch cognate, Genever, will only be discussed marginally. Secondly, although perhaps not completely scientifically correct, botanicals will be discussed generically in order to refer to all of the substances used to flavor gin, such as citrus fruits, spices and herbs, to name but a few. As far as the gin fact sheets are concerned, due to necessity we have only included thirty labels from the hundreds of references, which represent a large section of the heterogeneity of types, production methods, organoleptic characteristics, history and geography. Finally, the cocktails that are referred to are mostly inspired by the classics, some of which have existed since the dawn of mixed drinks in the 19th century, with the addition of a few modern interpretations.

6 • Miniature of a wine barrel from a 16th century copy of Pliny the Elder's Naturalis Historia.

History

Gin is a spirit, the origins of which lie in the alchemical corpus written by Jabir ibn Hayyan, or Geber depending on the Latinization of the name, which is based on alchemical and religious concepts. The history of gin starts here. It is the end of the 8th century, an era full of discoveries, a troubled era, and we are in Persia, where fractional distillation was born, described for the first time by Jabir ibn Hayyan. The key step was the transformation of the art of alchemy, which until then had been purely esoteric, into a successful book that made its way around the world. Although the distillation process was probably discovered on the Indian sub-continent in ancient times and for other purposes, it was this work, translated into several languages, which disseminated the methodology and alembic still in a form that is close to how we understand the process today. The spirit obtained from this process is magical, offering unlimited possibilities to the explorers of the time; possibilities that are taken advantage of in the form of a medicine, as this is was its end use. The explanation of the diseases was mainly based on the humoral theory of Hippocrates and Galen, according to which the purpose of medicine, as well as of food, was to balance the four basic humors in order to bring about what was defined as *eucrasia*. Much of Renaissance food was based on this theory and is also why spices, believed useful to stimulate "hot humor," were so sought after, to the point of giving decisive impetus to large shipping companies after the fall of Constantinople and the subsequent blocking of land routes for these precious raw materials.

9 • Jabir ibn Hayyan in a manuscript held
by the Laurentian Library in Florence.

The humoral theory resisted in several circles until the 17th century, slowly becoming obsolete with the arrival of the scientific method. The juniper plant has many valuable uses and is not limited to providing its berries for medicine. Its wood was used to produce boxes and barrels widely used, for example, in the production of traditional balsamic vinegar. The plant is also linked to the spirit in other ways: moonshiners loved using juniper wood, an excellent fuel with high calorific value which didn't emit smoke, thereby not making tax inspectors suspicious. The history of gin and its transformations began long before the beverage become what it is today.

The first distilled spirit made from juniper was probably Italic: the art of distillation moves to Salerno, where there is a fundamental school of medicine, the *Schola Medica Salernitana*, established in the 11th century and the most important medical institution in the Middle Ages, which, thanks to its contact with the Arab world, decisively promotes distillation in the West. The first documented example of a juniper-flavored beverage, which could be defined as a *proto-gin*, was in fact produced in Salerno. It is around the year 1000 and the Benedictine monks living here, who were probably the first to cultivate a botanical garden with the aim of extracting active plant ingredients, try to distill a spirit mixed with juniper for the very first time, with the intention of infusing the many beneficial properties of this plant, which was widespread in the area. The *Schola Medica Salernitana* mentions juniper-based anointing oil as a remedy against quartan fever, a fever that recurs intermittently every four days; this is also typical of malarial fever, which decisively crosses paths with the history of gin much later on.

The base ingredient for the production of alcohol was presumably grape, and it is very likely that the resulting product had basically the same aroma as a juniper grappa, but it is a key point in this story: juniper is added to the spirit; the instrument develops and disseminates; it travels through history with mixed fortunes to arrive as we know it in the present day. During this journey it meets a species of juniper that was subsequently pretty much forgotten: the Phoenician juniper (*Juniperus phoenicea*), found in southern Italy and Sardinia, with a different aromatic profile but the same medical characteristics.

The Year 1000 and the Beginning of a Geographical Journey

Gin begins its story as a juniper-based distillate in the Mediterranean, in around the year 1000, and then starts to move north, where it takes form and is improved on. The move is tinged with tragedy as its history entwines with the development of the plague across Europe. The Black Death, identified with the symbolic date of 1348, reduces the European population by at least a third and leaves its mark on history. Flemish alchemists

11 • Doctors of the Schola Medica Salernitana *treating Robert II, Duke of Normandy, who was wounded during the First Crusade. Miniature from a 14th century manuscript.*

also sing the praises of these berries. In his work *De Naturen Bloeme*, the great thirteenth-century poet Jacob van Maerlant recommends its use in various preparations, including boiling it in wine to treat an upset stomach and as a remedy to fight the increasingly common outbreaks of the Black Death. Doctors begin to understand contagion mechanisms and are convinced that the plague is hiding in the air. They decide to take advantage of the strong aromatic properties of the juniper plant to fumigate rooms; an attempt that was somewhere between ritual and empirical. Thanks to the diffusion of these fumigations and the juniper-based distillate, gin arrives in the Netherlands. In 1351, in his treatise on *aqua vitae*, Johannes de Aeltre wrote: "it makes us forget our sadness and turns us into happy and courageous people." Gin is no longer just a medicine.

Its journey across the Netherlands, which is at the center of large commercial networks and has a fervent cultural movement, is important not only for names and dates, but also because it is here that gin changes its aromatic profile; it is no longer just a medical instrument and its popularity rapidly increases. In the Netherlands gin meets a malt-based wine, *moutwijn*, and it also acquires another of its basic characteristics: it unites with the base alcohol. Because this is exactly what gin is, a marriage between a base alcohol and a recipe of herbs, roots and berries, celebrated by the alembic still. In 1552, Philippus Hermanni writes his treatise *Een Constelijck Distileerboec*, a detailed manual on distillation. In the same period, a wine shortage caused by bad harvest years and the decade-long war with Spain, which broke in 1568 for religious reasons, led to the introduction of cereals in the production of gin. After the war the Flemish region lost its strategic importance and the Netherlands was reorganized with the formation of the Dutch Republic, leading to many citizens of the kingdom to take refuge in England, taking the art of distillation with them. Up until 1606, spirits in the Flemish region were identified by the generic term "brandy," after which, with an act passed by the Dutch Republic, the term Genever was used, referred to and taxed like Brandy. The gin-based beverage became increasingly popular and starts to take on its own very distinct identity. Thanks to the dynamism of the East India Company, the wide availability of herbs and spices, up to then luxury goods, changes the profile of the beverages. *Genever* is a fundamental step in the journey towards modern gin. The Bols family, active in liquor production since 1575, adds Genever to its product range and, to ensure the availability of spices, becomes a shareholder of the East India Company. The availability of *moutwijn* in the Netherlands provides a starting point for arriving at today's gin, through the other great technical revolution of the 19th century: the column alembic still. This spirit is still on the market with the historic name Genever or Jenever, and is one of the precursors of gin that is still very much in vogue in modern mixed drinks.

The "British Fever" and Prerequisites for "Gin Dynasties"

The separation from its use as just a medical instrument starts to become clearer; history blends with legend and there is talk of the beverage instilling courage in the soldiers of William II of Orange during the Thirty Years War, which they drank before charging across the battlefield. Hence the famous phrase, Dutch Courage. Taking advantage of the war, a troubled succession to the throne and a conquest campaign, the effects of which are still evident in Northern Ireland, gin lands on the British Isles, arriving in London, where it continues its journey, once again with varying degrees of success. It is the 17th century, the New World has been discovered, trade routes are becoming more efficient and intercontinental trading has started. In 1688, William III becomes king of England and liberalizes the production of distillates. The upper classes continue to drink quality beverages, including Genever, while the poorer classes produce inferior imitations. Gin meets yet another plague, one that is even more devastating: alcoholism. It spreads quickly because of how easy the spirit is to produce. Gin become synonymous with a "mother's ruin." It is most likely an extremely poor quality gin, also produced with turpentine oil extracted from the resin of the plant, and at times lethal, but its diffusion among the hundreds of home distilleries is unstoppable. There are seven thousand places where it is served in London alone, including barber shops, and annual distillation in the capital is at around ten million gallons. Gin is the poor man's drink, in some cases used to pay wages for the equivalent of two pence a gallon; a gallon of beer costs a lot more, over four shillings. The government estimates the annual consumption per capita in London at about fourteen gallons, over sixty liters. The authorities try to stop this new plague with a set of laws, the Gin Acts. The Gin Act of 1751 coincides with the famous work *Beer Street* and *Gin Lane* by artist William Hogarth, in which he captures the virtues of beer and the miseries of gin.

Although gin consumption drops significantly, the first large family businesses start being established. In 1769, Alex Gordon starts producing gin in south London; James Stein produces *Dutch* gin in Scotland; and the Coates family opens its company in Plymouth. In 1825, the British government lowers taxes on gin, which, now less expensive, doubles consumption, exceeding seven million gallons, although still of very poor quality.

Gin is still being used as a medicine. On ships it is used to boost the diet of sailors; it is mixed with herbs that produce vitamins in the spirit, thereby obtaining a special and different aromatic profile. It has gone from being a simple medicine to a much enjoyed beverage, to improve on and to create with. Distilleries flourish and in this period gin begins to resemble the instrument we know today, being blended with botanicals that are still used, such as cardamom or coriander.

GIN LANE.

Gin cursed Fiend, with Fury fraught,
Makes human Race a Prey;
It enters by a deadly Draught,
And steals our Life away.

Virtue and Truth, driv'n to Despair,
It's Rage compells to fly,
But cherishes with hellish Care,
Theft, Murder, Perjury.

Damn'd Cup! that on the Vitals preys,
That liquid Fire contains,
Which Madness to the Heart conveys,
And rolls it thro' the Veins.

15 • *Mother's ruin depicted in Gin Lane by William Hogarth.*

A Fundamental Transition; the Birth of Gin & Tonic

Meanwhile, however, another momentous event is taking place elsewhere in the world: gin is embracing the quinine tree, and will remain united with it forever. The trade routes have met with a disease that needs to be treated, malaria, and a way to cure it has been found in a tree in South America, the properties of which are transmitted through an extremely bitter drink. The habit of mixing quinine with gin, in the form of "tonic water," took hold and Gin & Tonic was born; the backbone of the history of gin. In around the mid-1800s (between 1842 and 1847), about 700 tons of berries from quinine trees are being imported to India every year. This medicine, in itself costly because of the oceans the ingredients have to cross, finds its natural habitat in the circles of British Empire officers, therefore able to continue its journey from here. In 1858, the first industrial tonic water, a carbonated quinine-based drink, was patented and produced by Erasmus Bond. Gin comes into contact with aromas and spices from all over the world in alembic stills and glasses, becoming almost a symbol of the cosmopolitan colonial spirit. During the same period, distillation takes a decisive step towards today's gin.

Column Stills, Industrialization and the Big Brands

Between the 19th and early 20th century, gin is finally becoming that which we are familiar with today: the industrial revolution, the fine tuning of the art of distillation, ingredients from around the world and the tastes of far-sighted entrepreneurs all leave their mark, launching products that have proved themselves over the centuries and which are still on the crest of the wave today. With the introduction of the column still, the history of distillation continued pretty much in the same vein. The principle of distillation columns has already been grasped, but it is only in the 19th century that it is definitively industrialized, first by Rob-

17 • 19th century drawing of a column still.

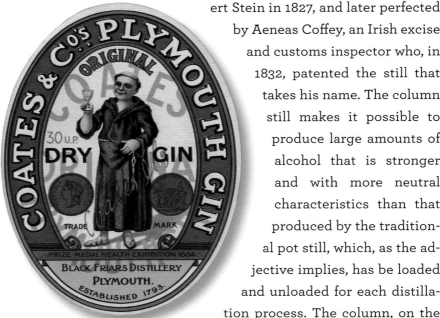

ert Stein in 1827, and later perfected by Aeneas Coffey, an Irish excise and customs inspector who, in 1832, patented the still that takes his name. The column still makes it possible to produce large amounts of alcohol that is stronger and with more neutral characteristics than that produced by the traditional pot still, which, as the adjective implies, has be loaded and unloaded for each distillation process. The column, on the other hand, uses a continuous distillation process and, thanks to a series of perforated plates inside the column, it "removes" a small amount of water and odorous and aromatic substances each time the vapor passes, gradually leaving an extremely pure distillate that is almost odorless and tasteless. This leads to the beginning of a different, lighter type of gin being produced, also because it is no longer necessary to use large amounts of botanicals to characterize the product and disguise the flavors and aromas of alcohol obtained by traditional and often rudimentary stills. It is was undoubtedly during this period that the various types of gin began to stand out more clearly from each other, with Dry Gin and Old Tom gin starting to go their separate ways. The latter is a much sweeter gin, more suited to drinking neat and in abundance. There is a story that tells how, in 1736, a certain Captain Dudley Bradstreet bought a store and put a cat in the window, from which, by putting a coin in, you could receive a shot of gin through a lead pipe. In the 1800s, the success of

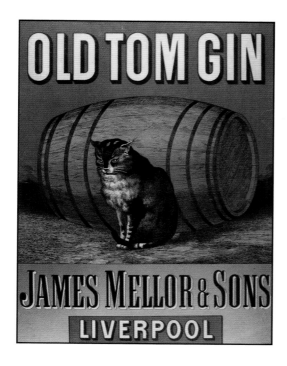

this initiative spread across London, and Old Tom cat became synonymous with gin.

With the new distillation techniques, the "Gin dynasties" and the big brands Booth's, Gordon's, Plymouth, Beefeater and Tanqueray put down their roots. The creation of the "cocktail" (in 1806, a mixture of distillate, water and bitters) and the "golden age," up until Prohibition in America during the 1930s, found a valuable and reliable partner in gin, which by now had a codified taste: the best British gins cross the Atlantic regularly, usually to be served by great bartenders in the United States of America. Here gin finds another of its fundamental characteristics: it becomes a distillate of multiple uses; a multi-purpose instrument. There are dozens of recipes for gin-based drinks from this period, which have now become classics. Gin elevates the aromatic notes of the other ingredients used: juniper is the trusted aide to bartenders' creativity, thanks to its characteristics and everything that it has become in the course of its journey.

America, Cocktails and Prohibition

America starts to produce its own gin due to the high demand for mixed drinks. In 1808, the Anchor Distillery starts producing gin. From the 1830s, with the industrialization of refrigeration, many people have access to ice. One of the first famous bartenders, Jerry Thomas, began to become known in the world of mixed drinks in the mid-1800s, and in 1862 he wrote what is perhaps the first book of cocktails. Old Tom and Genever are the protagonists of recipes during this period, while dry gin is rarely mentioned.

But times are changing, and in William Boothby's manual, written in 1908, dry gin starts to undermine other types. Prohibition pushes gin towards Canada and other illegal access points into the United States, as well as towards clandestine production and popular poor quality products. After Prohibition ends in 1933, gin enjoys huge popularity and the trend moves increasingly towards dry gin, while Old Tom is pretty much forgotten. Gin faces crisis after the Second World War, with the success of vodka, widely used in mixed drinks, which, thanks to its more neutral aromatic profile and lower cost, pushes gin aside, even in its homeland, England.

The End of the First Millennium of the History of Gin

Our journey has brought us to the end of the millennium, and over almost a thousand years gin has become an industry: huge companies offer strict, historicized products and between the changes in ownership of the "famous" distilleries, gin now marries the "market." Family businesses become part of the global market and the battle between the largest players in the market in the 1980s begins.

During this period a product that evokes gin's historical roots is created, one that quickly earns a place among the top brands in the world: Bombay Sapphire. The iconic nature of the immediately recognizable bottle, the perfect and balanced recipe and the production method – vapor infusion – which delicately extracts the aromas, guarantees its instant success.

The spirit's roots remain solid and certified, and gin continues its march along the curves of the sales charts, losing and gaining market shares, with four or five brands sharing most of the glory.

At this point something happens which will change history: small innovative producers slowly begin to appear, or "re-emerge." Historical recipes are revived and there is renewed interest in this distillate. We are now at the end of the 1990s: 1999 marks the birth of Hendrick's, an unequivocal sign that history is being changed once again. It proposes new distillation methods and new ingredients like rose and cucumber. In 2002, Tanqueray No. TEN is launched, with a recipe containing, perhaps for the first time, fresh citrus fruit.

20 • A happy-looking woman hugging bottles of spirits, including gin. One of the most well-known pictures of the Prohibition in America.

Gin Steps into the New Millennium with Grandiose and Tumultuous Prospects.

Gin has become a cereal-based spirit, distilled with juniper and other botanicals; it is cosmopolitan and multi-purpose, owned by large multinational companies. This is how gin enters its new era. Marketing firms, the growing global community of bartenders and internet guarantee its turning point. We see the launch of new products, advertised as "unusual," counterposing the centuries-old tradition, and at the same time small producers begin to emerge, able to arouse interest due to their pursuit of the highest possible quality.

We begin to see the geolocation of distilleries and recipes: in the first decade of the new millennium, gins that want to be characterized by their area of origin are launched on the market, with production methods that draw on history but with different ingredients to give them their own distinct characteristics: for example, going back to grapes for the base alcohol (as for G'Vine) or ingredients never used before, such as rosemary and olives (Gin Mare). The most forward-looking producers in this period of change already envisaged gin-based mixed drinks, which had lost their appeal and popularity, coming back into fashion.

We now arrive in a year to remember, 2008. The panorama has greatly changed in recent years, and the European Union decides to set regulations for the production of gin: the "gin dynasties" lose their battle for "London Dry" to only be produced on British soil, because it is now too widespread across the world to be downgraded to a local product. It is established that gin can also be produced in the European Union without distillation and without juniper as its base ingredient, through maceration and the use of extracts or concentrates: production is thereby facilitated and opens the way for many companies to produce infinite variations of gin.

Global Development

Gin begins to reach every corner of the globe. There is almost no country in the world without a distillery or its own gin brand. The short list of ingredients gets longer and longer, and includes strange and whimsical elements like algae, lichens, truffles and saffron.

This strengthens one of gin's historical characteristics: it is increasingly becoming more of a precision instrument. Once upon a time, a long list of cocktails just required the use of a good gin; today it is increasingly targeted and sophisticated, and the right gin is chosen for the right preparation. There are gins that are good for making a gin and tonic, but not a Martini. The research of bartenders, combined with the increasingly large number of producers on the market, pushes this trend for specialization even further, leading to almost surgical precision. The phenomenon which exploded on the Iberian Peninsula after 2008 is particularly interesting, with gin and tonic being revived by a few pioneers, leading to a full-on boom: it became the symbol of a moment of relaxation at the end of a workday. In many Spanish bars there are dozens of gins to choose from, all of which are mixed with specific tonic waters. In just a few years, Spain has become the biggest consumer of premium gins in the world, providing a big boost to research.

Tradition is being combined with constant innovation, which isn't always appreciated, but it has enlarged the gin family, increasing the possibilities that this spirit has to offer. Hundreds of brands popped up in the space of just a few years, each with a particular characterizing note that is able to clearly change the aromatic profile of a cocktail, offering a backbone to countless reinterpretations of the classics, to modernizations and at times even to a few adulterations. Gin is born and dies several times, coming back stronger, mutated, but always with solid roots which draw on each stage of its history.

Production

Gin is identified mainly by the ingredients that characterize it, the botanicals, which enrich a commonly neutral base alcohol. However, there are many ways to obtain gin, each of which may drastically change the profile and character, and they are also often used as a communication tool to claim uniqueness and differences when compared to the competition.

The Ingredients

The ingredients needed to produce gin, or more precisely the categories of ingredients, are basically three: alcohol, water and botanicals. Alcohol has the function of a "solvent" for extracting essential oils; botanicals provide odoriferous and aromatic substances; water is an essential "process" ingredient for bringing the alcohol to the desired strength during production.

The alcohol needed for the production of gin is usually distilled using column stills called Patent Stills, introduced in the first half of the 19th century. Alcohol obtained in this way, which has an alcohol content of approximately 95%, displays the aromas and flavors derived from the raw material used. Most producers use alcohol obtained from the distillation of cereals. Some gins, such as the French G'Vine, produced in the Cognac area, use distilled wines to differentiate the product, whereas Chase Elegant uses distilled cider.

Water is present in various stages of the production process and, in particular, used to dilute the product. Some producers use the origin of the water as a marketing tool and for brand differentiation. For example Martin Miller's displays the

Icelandic flag alongside the British one, because it is blended with *the purest Icelandic water.*

The Botanicals

Botanicals, which are the main differentiators between gins, are spices, herbs, roots, berries and, in general, products from the plant world that give the main scents, flavors and aromas to gin. The scents and aromas almost all come from the essential oils contained in the botanicals themselves.

Juniper

Juniper, *Juniperus communis*, grows in Europe, Asia and North America. The main production areas, also historically, are Tuscany and the whole of Central Italy. The Balkans, predominantly in Macedonia, and Scandinavia are also important areas. The age of the plants, the land and the freshness

 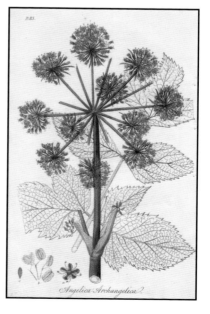

25 · Juniper (left) and Angelica (right) in a 19th century British study of officinal herbs.

of the product significantly affect the quality and quantity of essential oils contained in the berries. Juniper berries are the backbone of gin, infusing the balsamic and resinous notes of the conifers, eucalyptus, mint and camphor that are found in the woods where they grow.

Angelica

Angelica (*Angelica archangelica*), named so for the shape, is a plant belonging to the *Apiaceae* or *Umbelliferae* family, which includes carrots, celery, parsley, cumin and coriander, as well as hemlock. In herbal medicine it is well-known for its toning, anti-spasmodic and digestive properties.

It is widely cultivated in Northern Europe (Belgium, Germany, Hungary) and is often used in liquor; it is in fact a key ingredient in vermouths and Chartreuse.

The parts used for the production of gin are generally the

26 · Coriander (left) and iris (right) depicted in 20th century botanical tables.

dried roots, which provide hints of wild berries, soil and wood. It has a sweet taste and herbaceous and piney aromas can often be detected. The aromas of the seeds are reminiscent of juniper berries.

Coriander

Like Angelica, coriander (*Coriandrum sativum*) belongs to the *Apiaceae* family and is also known as coriander or Chinese parsley: mainly the seeds are used. The Latin name was given by Pliny the Elder and derives from the Greek words *corys* (stink bug) and *ander* (similar), due to the smell that the seeds and leaves give off if rubbed.

The essential oil is rich in *linalool*, an element that can also be found in high levels in lavender and basil, to name but two, and which is used abundantly in cosmetics. *Linalool* has predominantly floral scents and aromas, which are very fresh, with lemony notes.

Iris

The iris belongs to the Iridaceae family, which includes about 200 species. The name, of Greek origin, means rainbow and the flower is also known by the name *orris*. The roots, generally belonging to the *germanica* or *pallida* species, are used for the production of gin. It is widely cultivated in Italy and North Africa, but also in China and India. The iris has laxative and cleansing properties, as well as aiding digestion.

The root is dried, sometimes for long periods (24/36 months) and then made into a powder. It has more of a structural function than aromatic in the production of the gin; its essential oils act almost like a "ballast" for lighter and more volatile odorous and aromatic substances that would otherwise dissolve quickly. This is also why iris essential oil is widely used in the perfume industry, as well as for the root's typical violet note.

Citrus Fruits

Citrus fruits undoubtedly play a key role in modern gins. Lemon in particular enhances the notes of another widely used botanical, coriander. Modern gin recipes contain many types of citrus fruits: oranges, lime and bergamot, to name but a few.

Other Botanicals

Listing all of the botanicals used in the production of gin would be a difficult task. In addition to those listed, the following are also widely used: anise, mainly the *Pimpinella anisum*; cardamom (*Elettaria cardamomum*), which is also rich in linalool; cassia (*Cinnamomum cassia*), with its spicy, pungent, resinous and medicinal notes.

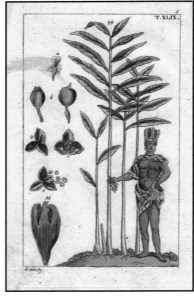

28 • Lemon (left) is widely used in modern gin recipes.
To the right, cardamom.

The Production Process

The differences between the production methods are primarily found in the method used to extract the aromatic substances from the botanicals.

The easiest way to obtain gin is through the "cold maceration" of the botanicals, namely immersing them in a mixture of water and alcohol or adding alcohol extracts. This method produces a cold compound gin. This is where the history of gins produced with hot infusion methods begins, namely distilled gins, which pass through the belly of an alembic still. Distillation has two main objectives: to concentrate the alcohol by eliminating part of the water and to extract the most volatile and aromatic elements from the botanicals.

Distillation is based on one simple principle: alcohol (ethanol) evaporates at a lower temperature than water, at about 78° C; by heating the water-alcohol solution, the alcohol is separated from the water, taking the most aromatic and volatile elements with it.

Alembic stills are not all the same: the two main categories are traditional pot stills (discontinuous stills) and column stills (Patent Still or Coffey Still). Over the course of time, stills have been perfected to take advantage of both principles, and as there are no restrictions, gins can be obtained in many different ways. It should be noted that if the base alcohol is obtained through column stills, the production of quality gin is oriented almost completely towards the use of pot stills.

Pot Still

We can think of a traditional alembic still as a large pot, which instead of a lid has a manifold, a swan neck, into which the vapors rise to be then conveyed to a cylinder containing water, and a condenser, which cools them down, allowing them to regain their liquid form.

The shape and proportions of the pot still's elements affect the final product. Low pot stills, typically "onion" shaped with a very wide, open neck, allow the heavier elements within the alcohol vapors to rise, thereby producing an oilier, richer and more aromatic alcohol. Tall pot stills, typically "pear" shaped with a narrow neck, stop the heavier elements in the vapor from rising and they fall back down, creating what is known as reflux; the higher the reflux ratio is, the lighter and more delicate the distilled alcohol will be. Pot stills are heated by steam or, very rarely, a naked flame, and they are made of copper due to the metal's ability to hold and remove elements that smell or taste bad during the distilling process, such as sulfur compounds.

Alembic Still with Vapor Extraction

These are pot stills with a perforated basket, filled with botanicals, attached to the swan neck. The alcohol vapors that pass through the basket extract the aromas from the botanicals; this technique is known as vapor infusion. The most famous of this type of still is the Carter-Head, named after its inventors, the Carter brothers, and it is used to produce, for example, Bombay Sapphire and Monkey 47.

Other Techniques

There are other distillation techniques which are combined with the previous ones or which use different technologies. There are stills which combine the principles of both column and traditional stills. They are still based on discontinuous distillation, but there is a column for obtaining a cleaner and lighter product. One of the most used models is the Holtein Still, used, for example, to produce Elephant Gin.

Vacuum distillation is another fairly widespread technique, which works on the principle that boiling occurs when the vapor pressure of a liquid exceeds the ambient pressure. The lower temperature allows the oils to be extracted more delicately, without the risk of cooking or burning the botanicals or changing their characteristics. Poli Marconi 46, Malfy and Sacred are among the producers that use this technique.

Blending and Bottling

Due to the variability of the botanicals' characteristics, many producers mix various batches together before bottling, in order to maintain a constant product. When this is not the case, it is often because a small batch process has been used; Tarquin's for example uses this type of distillation. There are also gins that are produced by distilling each botanical individually, and the various spirits are blended before bottling; Gin Mare is just one example of this.

The product then passes to the laboratory for analysis, the measurement of alcohol content and dilution. In many cases the product is chill filtered to remove any oily substances that could turn cloudy; some manufacturers choose not to filter the spirit, for example Hernö, and these are known as unchill-filtered or non chill-filtered products.

Reading the Labels and Applicable Regulations

Gin can be produced worldwide and there is not always a legislation to protect or regulate them. There is however an applicable legislation in the European Union (EC 110/2008), in which gin comes under spirits flavored with juniper (Juniperus communis), together with Genever and many of its regional variants. The legislation divides gin into two categories, depending on the production method – distilled or cold compounded – and it specifies that the minimum alcohol content in the bottle must be 37.5%. In the United States there is a similar legislation in the Code of Federal Regulations, which resembles that of the EU, although the minimum alcohol content is set at 80 proof (40%).

Around the World in 32 Gins

A Selection of Gin

The gins presented in detail have been grouped into three categories – traditional, contemporary and innovative – based on tradition, production methods and the botanicals used, trying, where possible, to contextualize them in terms of style or source of inspiration. The classification of gins is a fairly controversial topic, much discussed among experts, because the division of regulations, including where they exist, for example, in Europe and the United States, is rather generic and there is continuous innovation in styles, production methods and trends. The most famous or mainstream gins have been put among the most traditional ones, a few with variations or limited series, together with interpretations of traditional British styles. Among the contemporary gins are those which use unusual botanicals, often linked to the territory or which go hand-in-hand with recently developed trends. Innovative gins are produced with non-conventional methods and contain uncommon ingredients. Each gin is accompanied by historical and production information, serving suggestions and the recipe of a cocktail that enhances its characteristics.

Gin Tasting

In his collection of works on drinking, written in the early 1980s and brought together in the volume *Everyday Drinking: The Distilled*, Kingsley Amis was perhaps one of the first to rave about tasting "neat" gin in order to appreciate the essence of the botanicals. Gin is undoubtedly one of the kings of cocktails, although if you want to make the most of it, even in a cocktail, tasting it helps you to understand the structure, the potential and also any defects it may have. The first important thing is the glass, which has to be a tulip shaped copita, allowing you to direct the aromas towards the nose. The gin should be tasted at a temperature of 10-12°C so that you can smell the evolution as it warms. It is best to fill the glass up to its maximum width and to start smelling it by passing the nostrils quickly over the glass a few times. One of the greatest difficulties in tasting gin is in the volatility of some scents, which can be smelt immediately before they give way to those which are gradually more intense and complex. You may also find it difficult to recognize the scents and aromas that follow, as in many cases you may not be familiar with some of the botanicals; it's certainly not every day you get to smell cassia, Devil's Claw or angelica. Ideally you should build an olfactory memory by smelling as many ingredients as possible, and be able to tell the difference between natural scents and aromas and artificial ones. The first sip will serve to help your mouth adjust to the alcohol content. Take a few more short sips, holding the gin in your mouth for a few seconds each time: the heat in the mouth will release the underlying aromatic nose. Try to also smell with your mouth open; you'll notice how the different aeration tends to make the scents rise towards the top-up of the nose, as if it were a chimney. Adding a few drops of distilled water triggers chemical reactions that help to release a few other aromatic substances and, by lowering the alcohol content, can help in not overwhelming the mouth with alcohol. If you can't clearly identify the scents and aromas, try to classify them more generally in terms of the most common: balsamic and herbaceous notes of juniper, spice and citrus notes. Think about, for example, what type of tonic water or other aromas would pair well with it. Experimenting and comparing gins is the best way to learn.

Traditional Gins

Beefeater Burrough's Reserve

Bluecoat Barrel Reserve

Burleigh's Distiller's Cut

Cotswolds

Hayman's Old Tom

Jensen's Old Tom

Mayfair

No. 209

Plymouth Navy Strength

Star of Bombay

Tanqueray Bloomsbury Edition

Tarquin's

Vallombrosa Gin Dry

Using the British world as a point of reference for this classification, the gins which have a place of honor are those inspired by London Dry gins, the newfound popularity of Old Tom or the fascinating history of Plymouth Navy Strength. In gins inspired by tradition, juniper is the absolute protagonist, the recipes are fairly simple and the number and type of ingredients are limited. Great Britain holds its tradition proudly, both with historical brands like Tanqueray and new and recent products like Cotswolds and Tarquin's. Other important countries in the history of gin offer equally valid alternatives: the United States, with successful products like No. 209, and Italy, one of the leading suppliers of the highest quality juniper berries, also used by the monks at the Abbey of Vallombrosa, since the spirit's conception. Historic producers like Beefeater and newer ones like American Bluecoat, on the other hand, adhere to the tradition of barrel-aged gins, a practice that was originally used when this spirit was stored and transported in wooden crates.

Style: *Dry Gin aged in barrels/traditional*
Country: *UK*
ABV: *43%*
Bottle: *70 cl*

Production: *traditional copper pot still.*
Botanicals: *juniper, orange peel, coriander, almonds, lemon peel, iris, angelica, licorice.*

The origins of Beefeater date back to 1863, when James Burrough, a pharmacist by profession, bought the Taylor distillery in London. The brand was launched thirteen years later and the distillery remained in the family until 1987. Beefeater Burrough's Reserve is produced using James Burrough's original recipe from 1860, and is distilled in the original copper "Still number 12," with a 268 liter capacity. The small batches that are placed on the market are aged in different types of barrels, indicated on the label. The first edition was produced by aging the gin in French barrels which had previously contained Lillet, a famous aromatized French wine flavored mainly with citrus fruits and quinine: the second edition was aged in barrels previously used for Bordeaux wine. The Beefeater range of gins also includes the classic dry gin Beefeater 24, which contains different types of tea, and London Garden. Master Distiller Desmond Payne is undoubtedly one of the most well-known figures in the world of gin.

Tasting
Nose: *spice notes of wood, juniper and lemon.*
Palate: *herbaceous and balsamic, wood, spices, red berries and licorice.*
Finish: *long, spicy and complex.*
Ideal: *neat.*

Gin Old Fashioned

45 ml (1 1/2 fl oz) Beefeater Burrough's Reserve • 2 dashes of Angostura •
1 sugar cube • A splash of soda

Method: build • Glass: old fashioned
Garnish: slice of orange and a Maraschino cherry

Put the sugar cube on a napkin and soak it with Angostura. Put it in an old fashioned glass and add a little natural mineral water, stirring until the sugar cube dissolves. Fill the glass with ice cubes, add the gin and stir. Garnish with a slice of orange and a Maraschino cherry.

Bluecoat Barrel Reserve

Style: *barrel-aged/traditional*
Country: *USA*
ABV: *47%*
Bottle: *70 cl*

Production: *traditional copper pot stills.*
Botanicals: *juniper, coriander, lemon, angelica.*

Created in Philadelphia in 2006, Bluecoat Gin is a tribute to America and the uniform worn by soldiers during the American War of Independence, in the city where it was declared. Bluecoat is produced using only certified organic botanicals, and is the result of five slow distillation processes which produce a smooth and well-balanced artisan gin. The producer chose a recipe with few ingredients, skillfully heightening the notes of the same in pursuit of the highest possible quality.

This version of Bluecoat Gin that is aged in American oak barrels, creating a complex and smooth gin, is ideal for recipes which originally used whisky or bourbon.

Tasting

Nose: *evident citric notes of lemon.*
Palate: *smooth, citric and spicy.*
Finish: *dry, fresh and clean.*
Ideal: *in a Tom Collins.*

The Income Tax

50 ml (1 3/4 fl oz) Bluecoat Barrel Reserve Gin • 20 ml (2/3 fl oz) sweet vermouth • 20 ml (2/3 fl oz) dry vermouth • 15 ml (1/2 fl oz) orange juice • 2 dashes Angostura

Method: shake&double strain • Glass: cocktail • Garnish: orange peel twist

Put the ingredients in a shaker and shake vigorously. Use a sieve to pour the drink into a chilled cocktail glass and garnish with an orange peel twist.

Burleigh's

LONDON DRY
GIN

DISTILLER'S CUT

MADE IN ENGLAND

70CL℮ 47%VOL

Burleigh's Distiller's Cut

Style: *Dry Gin/traditional*
Country: *UK*
ABV: *47%*
Bottle: *70 cl*

Production: *Holstein copper pot stills.*
Botanicals: *juniper, angelica, orris, coriander, cassia, silver birch, cardamom, elderberries, orange peel, dandelion, burdock.*

Burleigh's Distiller's Cut is the creation of Master Distiller Jamie Baxter, in which he has expressed his personal taste and philosophy. The distillery is situated in the heart of England, in Charnwood Forest in Leicestershire. Distiller's Cut uses the base of dry gin, changing the concentration of the botanicals, modifying the cut points in the distillation run and bottling with a higher alcohol content. The gin is produced by a 450-liter Holstein still called Messy Bessy.

Tasting

Nose: *delicate with juniper, eucalyptus and lemon notes.*
Palate: *smooth and dry, savory and spicy.*
Finish: *dry, floral and aromatic.*
Ideal: *in a Martinez or Gin & Tonic with Fever Tree Premium Indian tonic.*

Sweet Selmer Cocktail

25 ml (2/3 fl oz) Burleigh's Distiller's Cut • 25 ml (2/3 fl oz) Lillet Blanc • 20 ml (2/3 fl oz) lemon juice • 15 ml (1/2 fl oz) honey syrup

Method: shake&strain • Glass: coupe • Garnish: an edible flower and a pink grapefruit twist

To make the honey syrup, just add water to the honey and stir until it has completely dissolved. Put the ingredients in a shaker with ice and shake for at least 10 seconds. Pour into a chilled martini glass and complete with a pink grapefruit twist. Garnish with an edible flower, for example a pansy.

Cotswolds

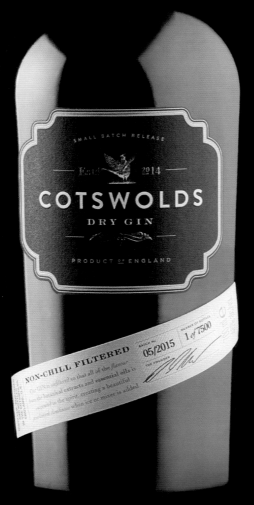

Style: *Dry Gin/ traditional*
Country: *UK*
ABV: *46%*
Bottle: *70 cl*

Production: *Holstein copper pot still.*
Botanicals: *coriander, cardamom, black pepper, juniper, lavender, angelica, bay leaf, lime and grapefruit.*

Cotswolds is produced in Stourton, a village in Wiltshire that lies at the foot of the Cotswold Hills. The distillery was founded in 2014 by Dan Szor, a powerful man in the financial world who loves getting out of London at the weekends to enjoy the peace of the English countryside. Szor had the insight to use the local grain crops grown to produce whisky for the production of this gin. The distillery controls the entire production process, from malting the cereals right through to the final product. The gin is produced with a hybrid Holstein still, which is used to both macerate the botanicals, for about 12 hours, and for vapor infusion, through the use of a basket inserted into the top of the still's neck and filled with the botanicals.

Tasting
Nose: *intense, persistent with lavender floral notes.*
Palate: *predominant grapefruit note.*
Finish: *persistent and fresh.*
Ideal: *on the rocks, in an Aviation or Ramos Gin Fizz.*
Try to pair the lavender notes when mixing.

UK Pic Nic

50 ml (1 3/4 fl oz) Cotswolds Gin • 15 ml (1/2 fl oz) red berry shrub • 5 ml (1/6 fl oz) grenadine • Fresh raspberries and wild strawberries

Method: Build • Glass: highball or Collins
Top-up: Prosecco or Blanquette De Limoux • Garnish: sprig of mint

Crush the red berries with a pestle to create a puree and put all the ingredients in a shaker with ice. Shake vigorously and pour into the glass; top up with Prosecco or Blanquette De Limoux. Garnish with a sprig of mint. To make the shrub, mix equal parts fruit and sugar and leave for a few days. Crush the fruit to release all of the juice and filter into a container. Add red wine or apple cider vinegar, the acidifying ingredient, and put in the refrigerator. Alternatively, you can make a syrup by heating water, sugar and fruit in a pan; leave it to cool and then add vinegar to taste.

Hayman's
Old Tom

Style: *Old Tom Gin/traditional*
Country: *UK*
ABV: *40%*
Bottle: *70 cl*
Production: *copper still.*
Botanicals: *Bulgarian and Macedonian juniper berries, Bulgarian coriander seeds, nutmeg from India, Madagascan cinnamon, orange peel from Spain, Belgian or French angelica root, Italian orris root, Chinese cassia bark, Sri Lankan licorice, Spanish lemon peel.*

Christopher Hayman, the founder of the distillery, boasts a long tradition in distilling, as he is a direct descendant of James Burrough, who founded Beefeater Gin in 1863.

Christopher began his career at James Burrough Ltd. in 1969, and was responsible for the distillation and production of Beefeater Gin until 1988, leaving when the company passed into the hands of a big multinational.

Hayman's was probably the first distillery to revive the tradition of Old Tom after its rebirth as a modern gin. Hayman's Old Tom Gin is distilled with an original recipe used by the Burrough family in 1870. Old Tom was a style of gin that was extremely popular when cocktails first appeared in the 1800s, and it appears in several cocktails listed in the famous *Bartenders Guide* by Jerry Thomas (1886), although over time it was replaced by dry gin.

Tasting
Nose: *lemon, almond, ginger, chocolate and coffee notes with a hint of herbs.*
Palate: *smooth and round with floral and citrus notes and a typical sweet finish.*
Finish: *balsamic and spicy.*
Ideal: *in a Tom Collins and a Ramos Gin Fizz.*

Gin Martinez

25 ml (2/3 fl oz) Hayman's Old Tom Gin • 50 ml (1 3/4 fl oz) Italian red Vermouth •
2 dashes of Maraschino liqueur • 1 dash of orange bitters

Method: stir&strain • Glass: martini • Garnish: lemon twist

Put all of the ingredients in a mixing glass with ice and stir. Pour into a chilled martini glass and garnish with a lemon twist. The alternative is to make a syrup by boiling water, sugar and fruit in a pan; allow to cool and then add vinegar to taste.

jensen's

When Christian Jensen
first tasted the vintage
gins from London's lost
distilleries, he began
a journey. Creating a
finely balanced gin that
honoured these forgotten
recipes became his
obsession. That's why
Jensen's is distilled in
small batches, using only
traditional gin botanicals.
So there's really nothing
new about Jensen's, and
that's why it's different.
Distilled in Bermondsey,
London, Jensen's is gin as
it was. Gin as it should be.

**LONDON DISTILLED
OLD TOM GIN**

70CL 43% VOL.

Jensen's Old Tom

Style: *Old Tom/traditional*
Country: *UK*
ABV: *43%*
Bottle: *70 cl*

Production: *John Dore & Co. copper stills*
Botanicals: *unspecified classic ingredients.*

Jensen's gin is one of the symbols of the revival of British gin. The distillery opened in 2013 and is housed in an old railway arch at Bermondsey, from which the distillery takes its name. The owners' idea was to produce a distillate based on tradition, although combined with state-of-the-art technology. The 500-liter still was built by John Dore & Co, founded by Aeneas Coffey in 1830. One of the distinguishing characteristics of this distillery is the presence of a female Master Distiller with a degree in chemistry, Anne Brok. Old Tom is produced without sweeteners, using a recipe from 1840, with the aim of faithfully reconstructing the gin as it was drunk at the time. The product line also includes a dry gin.

Tasting
Nose: *fresh balsamic notes.*
Palate: *fresh juniper and conifer notes.*
Finish: *spicy, balsamic and vegetal.*
Ideal: *in a Ramos Gin Fizz, Martinez or a Tom Collins.*

Black Cat

30 ml (1 fl oz) Jensen's Old Tom • 30 ml (1 fl oz) mezcal • 25 ml (2/3 fl oz) Amontillado sherry • 25 ml (2/3 fl oz) Punt e Mes Carpano • 1 tbsp sugar syrup (ratio water/sugar 1:1) • 1 grapefruit twist

Method: stir&strain • Glass: martini • Garnish: slice of grapefruit peel

Mix the slice of grapefruit peel and the syrup in a mixing glass together with ice. Add the other ingredients and stir. Pour into a chilled martini glass and garnish with a slice of grapefruit peel.

Mayfair

Style: *Dry Gin/traditional* **Production:** *traditional copper pot stills.*
Country: *UK* **Botanicals:** *juniper, angelica, iris,*
ABV: *40%* *coriander, savory and other unspecified*
Bottle: *70 cl* *botanicals.*

Mayfair Gin is an example of a modern gin that revives tradition and history. The Master Distiller comes from a family with over three centuries of experience in the world of distillation. The brand was created by four businessmen, who focused greatly on brand communication in order to position it as a luxury brand. The distillery has two copper stills, called Tom Thumb and Thumbelina. The first, with a capacity of 500 liters, is used to produce gin, while the second is used for vodka. As well as gin and vodka, the product line also includes a rum.

Tasting
Nose: *juniper and conifers and a lemon note.*
Palate: *smooth and full-bodied with evident juniper.*
Finish: *dry with lemon and coriander notes.*
Ideal: *in Negroni.*

The Mayfair Elegance

35 ml (1 1/6 fl oz) Mayfair Gin • 50 ml (1 3/4 fl oz) Jasmine tea with honey •
15 ml (1/2 fl oz) Chartreuse Jaune

Method: stir&strain • Glass: old fashioned
Garnish: slice of orange peel and violet

Mix the ingredients together in a mixing glass with some ice. Pour into an old fashioned glass full of ice and garnish with a slice of orange peel and a violet.

No. 209

Style: *Dry Gin/traditional*
Country: *USA*
ABV: *46%*
Bottle: *70 cl*
Production: *traditional copper still.*

Botanicals: *Calabrian juniper, bergamot orange, lemon, cardamom, cassia, angelica, coriander and other unspecified ingredients.*

No. 209 Gin is a distillate made in the USA, produced in California by one of the distilleries that has driven the gin movement on this continent. The name comes from the identification number listed in the U.S. registers for the historic distillery that the Rudd family, which also owns many vineyards, decided to reopen in 2000, moving its premises near the pier of San Francisco and producing the first gin in 2005. The copper still was produced in Scotland, inspired by that of the Glenmorangie distillery in terms of its shape and height, over eight meters high, and it is capable of producing an extremely light distillate. The Rudd family's connection to the world of Californian wine is evident from the range of No. 209 products: there are three barrel-aged variations (Sauvignon, Cabernet and Chardonnay), all coming from vineyards in the Napa Valley. The product line also includes a gin and vodka which are Kosher certified.

Tasting

Nose: *predominant pine notes of juniper, followed by a scent of cedar wood.*
Palate: *balance between the fresh notes of juniper and conifers and all the other ingredients in the recipe, in particular the citrus fruits.*
Finish: *smooth and decisive with a coriander and licorice note.*
Ideal: *in Martini cocktail.*

Red Zone

30 ml (1 fl oz) No. 209 Gin • 120 ml (4 fl oz) cranberry juice • 60 ml (2 fl oz) ginger ale

Method: shake&strain • Glass: old fashioned
Top-up: ginger ale • Garnish: slice of orange

Put the gin and cranberry juice in a shaker and shake. Pour into an old fashioned glass with ice. Top up with ginger ale and garnish with a slice of orange.

Plymouth
Navy
Strength

Style: *Navy Strength/traditional*	**Production:** *traditional copper pot stills.*
Country: *UK*	**Botanicals:** *juniper, coriander, lemon and*
ABV: *57%*	*orange peel, angelica, iris, cardamom.*
Bottle: *70 cl*	

Plymouth was founded in 1793 and was known as Coates & Co, after its founder. Given the geographical location, the connection between Plymouth and the British Royal Navy dates back more than two centuries, linking it also to one of the most well-known British flag officers in the Royal Navy, Lord Nelson. During the battles against Napoleon, Nelson loaded his ships with barrels of Plymouth for his officers; this gin became known as Navy Strength due to its high alcohol content. But why did he choose a gin with an alcohol content of over 57 degrees, also called 100 proof? Imagine the stormy sea or the firing of a cannon and a barrel of gin that breaks and drenches the gunpowder; empirically gunpowder wet by a gin with less than 100 proof would become unusable. This is how the Navy Strength myth was born: in the mid-19th century, the distillery provided the navy with about one thousand barrels a year. After years of decline and oblivion, with recipes being changed and alcohol content reduced, Plymouth was reborn in 1996 thanks to Charles Rolls. Currently, the distillery is owned by a big multinational company.

Tasting
Nose: *juniper and lemon.*
Palate: *fresh with notes of aromatic herbs and flowers.*
Finish: *long, balsamic and with citrus notes.*
Ideal: *in Gin & Tonic with a slice of lime or in a Gimlet.*

The Pink Gin

60 ml (2 fl oz) Plymouth Navy Strength · 1 dash of Angostura

Method: stir&strain · Glass: martini · Garnish: lemon twist

Put the Angostura bitters in a mixing glass full of ice and stir for about fifteen seconds. Pour into a martini glass and "dirty" the sides with it. Turn the glass to eliminate any excess liquid. Pour the gin on to the ice left in the mixing glass and allow it to dilute until the alcohol is less aggressive; pour into the previously prepared glass. Add a lemon twist and garnish.

Star of Bombay

Style: *Dry Gin/traditional*
Country: *UK*
ABV: *47.5%*
Bottle: *70 cl*
Production: *Carter-Head pot still using vapor infusion.*

Botanicals: *juniper, lemon peel, grains of paradise, coriander, Giava pepper, florentina iris, almonds, cassia, licorice, angelica, Calabrian bergamot orange peel, Ecuadoran ambrette.*

The launch of Bombay Sapphire on the market in 1987 most definitely marks a watershed in the history of modern gin, decreeing the rebirth of a delicate style of gin, made unique by its blue sapphire bottle.
The Bombay Sapphire recipe was one of the first to be registered and dates back to 1761, thanks to the work of Thomas Dakin who founded one of the largest distilleries outside London.
Star of Bombay, named after a 182-carat sapphire kept at the Smithsonian Institution, uses the same base as Bombay Sapphire with the addition of two botanicals: Calabrian bergamot orange peel and Ecuadoran ambrette seeds. The alcohol content was increased and the vapor infusion process slowed down, thereby extracting more essential oils and aromas.

Tasting

Nose: *intense with coriander, angelica, lemon and juniper notes.*
Palate: *aromatic and very floral, with citrus, spice and licorice notes.*
Finish: *balsamic and spicy with licorice notes.*
Ideal: *in Gin&Soda to enhance the aromatic notes of the herbs and citrus fruits.*

Intense Gin & Tonic

Star of Bombay and Tonic, preferably with floral aromas, in equal parts.

Method: build · Glass: highball · Garnish: slice of bergamot peel

Pour the ingredients straight into a highball glass filled with ice and stir. Garnish with a slice of bergamot orange peel.

Tanqueray Bloomsbury Edition

Style: *Dry Gin/traditional*
Country: *UK*
ABV: *47.3%*
Bottle: *100 cl*

Production: *copper stills.*
Botanicals: *Italian juniper, coriander, angelica and savory.*

Tanqueray Bloomsbury is a limited edition gin based on a recipe from 1880: in fact the wealth of the great "gin dynasties" lies in their historical archives, a rich source of recipes to reinterpret, and it is from here that a simple yet rich gin begins its life. The name comes from the London borough where the Tanqueray distillery was located at the time. The label displays the simple recipe of this juniper-based gin; the plant's origin is also indicated to pay homage to ancient traditions which link this Italian plant with British gin. Bloomsbury is part of a series of Tanqueray gins produced in limited editions, based on historical recipes, which time after time enhance a particular characteristic and offer an almost perfect vision of gin in that particular era.

Tasting

Nose: *predominant juniper, spices and flowers.*
Palate: *juniper, coriander and savory.*
Finish: *long and clean.*
Ideal: *in a Martini cocktail with a slice of lemon peel.*

Tuxedo

30 ml (1 fl oz) Tanqueray Bloomsbury gin • 30 ml (1 fl oz) dry Vermouth •
2.5 ml (1/12 fl oz) Maraschino liqueur • 1.25 ml (1/24 fl oz) absinthe •
3 drops of orange bitter

Method: stir&strain • Glass: cocktail
Garnish: lemon peel twist and a Maraschino cherry

Mix the ingredients in a mixing glass with lots of ice. Pour into a chilled cocktail glass and complete with a lemon twist. Garnish with a Maraschino cherry inside a lemon peel spiral.

Tarquin's

Style: *Dry Gin/traditional*
Country: *UK*
ABV: *42%*
Bottle: *70 cl*
Production: *traditional copper pot stills.*

Botanicals: *juniper, coriander seeds, orange peel, lemon, grapefruit, angelica roots, cinnamon, licorice, Devon violets and other unspecified ingredients.*

Tarquin's is distilled by the Southwestern Distillery in Cornwall, which revived a tradition that had been lost for over a century. The gin is produced in a very small copper still, called Tamara, which produces single batches of just three hundred bottles, all of which are labeled, numbered and signed by hand. A cereal alcohol base is used and the water used for dilution has been very carefully chosen, hailing from a spring near Boscastle. Interestingly, the distillery also produces Pastis, inspired by the French tradition.

Tasting
Nose: *juniper, citrus fruits, cinnamon and a violet floral note.*
Palate: *spices, citrus fruits.*
Finish: *dry and spicy.*
Ideal: *in Gin & Tonic, ratio gin to tonic 1:4, lots of ice and a slice of lemon.*

Cornish Martini

50 ml (1 3/4 fl oz) Tarquin's Gin • 10 ml (1/3 fl oz) dry Vermouth • 1 drop of Pastis

Method: stir&strain • Glass: martini • Garnish: lemon twist

Pour the ingredients into a mixing glass together with ice and stir.
Pour into a chilled martini glass and add a lemon twist.

GIN DRY
VALLOMBROSA

ALCOLATO DI BACCHE DI GINEPRO
SECONDO LE ANTICHE RICETTE DEI
MONACI BENEDETTINI DI **VALLOMBROSA** · FIRENZE

LICENZA U.T.I.F FIX00007S - TRASF. A FREDDO
cl 70   GRADI 47

Vallombrosa Gin Dry

Style: *Dry Gin/traditional*
Country: *Italy*
ABV: *47%*
Bottle: *70 cl*

Production: *maceration in alcohol.*
Botanicals: *Juniper and other native herbs.*

The abbey of Vallombrosa, situated in the Tuscan-Emilian Appenines at 1000 meters above sea level, stands in an ancient forest and was originally built in 1028 by San Giovanni Gualberto; the present buildings are from the 15th century. It was abandoned during the Napoleonic period and after it was returned to the monks in 1949, the Benedictines began extensive restoration works. Vallombrosa Dry Gin is produced with a single wild variety of juniper berries that grows on the hills between Sansepolcro and Pieve Santo Stefano, in the province of Arezzo, discovered in the period during which the monks carried out forest recovery activities for the Forestry Corps. The highly aromatic characteristic of this variety of berries can be fully appreciated in the finished product.

Tasting

Nose: *fresh and intense, predominant juniper.*
Palate: *herbaceous and juniper notes, sweet.*
Finish: *dry, balsamic with herby notes, very persistent and aromatic.*
Ideal: *neat, to fully appreciate the juniper notes, in Gin & Tonic or a Martini cocktail.*

Gin Sour

60 ml (2 fl oz) Vallombrosa dry gin • 25 ml (2/3 fl oz) lemon juice • 25 ml (2/3 fl oz) sugar syrup

Method: shake&strain • Glass: Coupette • Garnish: sage leaves

Put all the ingredients in a shaker, add ice and shake. Pour into a chilled Coupette and garnish with sage leaves.

Contemporary Gins

Bulldog

Caorunn

Elephant Gin

Hernö Juniper Cask Gin

Juniper Green Trophy

Martin Miller's 9 Moons

Shortcross

Skin Gin

The Botanist

Ungava

Williams Elegant Chase

The world of gin has changed and expanded significantly over the past two decades. Returning to tradition was one of the inspirations for rekindling consumer interest, but it didn't take long for new products with a more modern edge to appear; modernized recipes, the latest production methods and new marketing strategies, with increasingly unusual and imaginative bottles and labels, together with targeted communication to highlight all these characteristics. The solid foundation of contemporary gins lies in tradition, but producers were able to skillfully introduce elements of differentiation, for example, unusual, local or exotic ingredients. Caorunn and The Botanist are born from the tradition of Scottish whiskey distilleries, but they have introduced a large number of local and long forgotten botanicals, such as the Coul Blush apple. The German Elephant Gin is inspired by Africa, both in its ingredients and communication campaigns focused on the preservation of the large mammal, to which it greatly contributes. The Swedish gin Hernö is probably the first commercial product to be aged in barrels made from much-prized juniper wood, while Chase makes gin with alcohol made from apples that the same company produces.

BULLDOG

A Brazen Breed,
Perfectly Balanced With
Natural Poppy, Dragon Eye
And Hints Of Crisp Citrus.
Bulldog Guards The Time-Honoured
Tradition Of Distilling,
Meeting All Opposition With
Brilliant Character And
A Palatable Disposition.

Respect Its Spirit And
It Will Remain Forever Loyal

LONDON DRY GIN
DISTILLED FROM 100% GRAIN NEUTRAL
PRODUCT OF ENGLAND
40% VOL   70 cl

Bulldog

Style: *London Dry Gin/contemporary*
Country: *UK*
ABV: *40%*
Bottle: *70 cl*
Production: *traditional copper pot stills.*

Botanicals: *Tuscan juniper, iris, Moroccan coriander, Spanish lemons, French lavender, lotus leaves, licorice, poppy, Longan.*

Bulldog is the brainchild of American Anshuman Vohra, who founded the brand with the name of a well-known British dog breed, also chosen in honor of Dog of the Year 2006, the year in which the brand was founded. The ingredients are fairly traditional except for the addition of Longan fruit, also known as Dragon Eye, a fruit from China similar to a litchi.
The gin is produced with a traditional method in a large London distillery and is distilled four times. There is also a Bold version with a higher alcohol content.

Tasting
Nose: *juniper and floral notes of lavender.*
Palate: *floral, fruity with balsamic and licorice notes.*
Finish: *spicy, balsamic and dry.*
Ideal: *in Gin & Tonic with a sprig of lavender to garnish.*

Southside

60 ml (2 fl oz) Bulldog gin • 30 ml (1 fl oz) lemon juice • 5 small mint leaves • 25 ml (2/3 fl oz) sugar syrup

Method: shake&double strain • Glass: old fashioned
Garnish: sprig of mint

Put the ingredients in a shaker with ice and shake vigorously. Pour into an old fashioned glass with ice, using a sieve, and garnish with a sprig of mint.

CAORUNN★

Stèidhichte
{ 1824 }

*Handcrafted from pure
grain spirit and time-honoured
Celtic botanicals.*

CAORUNN
ka-roon

CAORUNN

{ka-roon}

Caorunn

Style: *Dry Gin/contemporary*
Country: *UK/Scotland*
ABV: *41.8%*
Bottle: *70 cl*
Production: *Berry Chamber copper still.*

Botanicals: *juniper, coriander seeds, lemon peel, orange peel, angelica, cassia, rowan berries, Bog myrtle (Myrica gale), heather, dandelion, Coul Blush apple.*

Carounn is produced at the Balmenach Distillery, using the only known example of a working Berry Chamber copper still. This type of still was widely used in the 1900s and enables the aromas to be extracted slowly and delicately. The botanicals are placed inside a basket that is divided into four compartments, and as the distillation vapors slowly rise, they gently take the aromatic components with them.

The gin is produced in small batches of around one thousand liters. Carounn is the Gaelic name for rowan berries, the fruit of a species of mountain ash growing in many areas of northern Europe. One of the botanicals is a fairly unknown and forgotten variety of apple, the Coul Blush.

Tasting
Nose: *floral with white berry and juniper notes.*
Palate: *sweet and extremely velvety with an apple note.*
Finish: *fresh and dry.*
Ideal: *in Gin & Tonic garnished with slices of Pink Lady apple.*

Chilli and Mandarin Collins

25 ml (2/3 fl oz) Caorunn Gin • 25 ml (2/3 fl oz) Mandarine Napoleon • 25 ml (2/3 fl oz) lemon juice • 7.5 ml (1/4 fl oz) gum syrup • Half a chilli pepper, roughly chopped

Method: shake&double strain • Glass: Collins • Top-up: soda
Garnish: chilli pepper

Put the ingredients in a shaker with ice and shake. Sieve into the glass and add crushed ice. Top up with soda and garnish with a chilli pepper.

Elephant Gin

Style: *Dry Gin/contemporary*
Country: *Germany*
ABV: *45%*
Bottle: *70 cl*
Production: *Holstein copper pot still.*

Botanicals: *juniper, mountain pine needles, lavender, sweet orange peel, fresh apple, cassia bark, ginger, pimento berries, Devil's Claw, Buchu, elderflower, Lion's Tail, African wormwood, baobab.*

The distillery is situated outside Hamburg and uses Holstein copper stills. The botanicals, some of which are of African origin, are macerated for about twenty-four hours. The recipe is inspired by London Dry Gin and before bottling the distillate is left to rest for several days. The gin is produced in small batches of about 700 bottles each. Each batch takes its name from an elephant and 15% of the profits go towards the protection of the African elephant, through the Big Life Foundation and Space for Elephants. The founders say the idea of a gin inspired by Africa came from the *sundowner*, the generic name used in South Africa for a drink that you sip at sunset after a hard day's work.

Tasting

Nose: *predominant note of fresh juniper and conifers accompanied by a strong hint of apple.*
Palate: *smooth, floral and fruity with a predominant flavor of apple.*
Finish: *spicy.*
Ideal: *in Gin & Tonic with slices of ginger and apple.*

Wild Freedom

*50 ml (1 3/4 fl oz) Elephant Gin • 30 ml (1 fl oz) lime juice • 15 ml (1/2 fl oz) ginger syrup •
15 ml (1/2 fl oz) Chartreuse Jaune • 3 drops of rosemary tincture
(1 part fresh rosemary to 2 parts alcohol, left to macerate for 3 days)*

Method: shake&strain • Glass: Coupette • Garnish: sprig of rosemary

Put the ingredients in a shaker with ice and shake. Pour into a chilled Coupette and garnish with a sprig of rosemary on the rim of the glass.

Hernö Juniper Cask Gin

Style: *barrel-aged/contemporary*
Country: *Sweden*
ABV: *47%*
Bottle: *50 cl*
Production: *traditional copper pot stills.*

Botanicals: *Bulgarian juniper and coriander, lemon, Swedish lingonberries, Madagascan vanilla, Indonesian cassia, Indian black pepper, British meadowsweet flowers.*

The first Swedish distillery dedicated exclusively to gin was founded by Jon Hillgren in 2011. It is in Dala, on the outskirts of Härnösand, in a region called *High Coast*, which is a UNESCO World Heritage site. The distillery is housed in a traditional red and white wooden building. They use two copper stills, nicknamed Kerstin and Marit, and all the types of gin produced have a base of eight botanicals, all of which are organic. This product, like all those produced by the distillery, is non-chill filtered. The product line also includes Dry Gin, Navy Strength, Old Tom, Juniper Cask ages for thirty days in juniper wood barrels of 39.25 liters.

Tasting

Nose: *intense, moss, cut grass, juniper and conifer notes.*
Palate: *sweet, dry, intense and persistent with coniferous and citric notes.*
Finish: *dry, balsamic with a pine resin and juniper note.*
Ideal: *in Gin & Tonic with fresh coriander and lime.*

Juniper Cask Tonic

50 ml (1 3/4 fl oz) Hernö Juniper Cask Gin • 150 ml (5 fl oz) tonic

Method: build • Glass: balloon • Garnish: juniper berries, dried black olives and dried bay leaves.

Pour the ingredients into a balloon glass filled with ice and stir. Garnish with juniper berries, dried black olives and dried bay leaves. It is best to use a dry tonic.

Juniper Green Trophy

Style: *Organic Dry Gin/contemporary*
Country: *UK*
ABV: *43%*
Bottle: *70 cl*

Production: *traditional copper pot stills.*
Botanicals: *juniper, coriander, angelica, savory.*

Juniper Green Trophy has been on the market since 1999, and, while not investing much in advertising, earned acclaim by aiming to offer a distillate that was certified at every stage; the grain used to produce the base alcohol is biodynamic; the cultivated botanicals are organic and the wild ones have a certificate ensuring that the natural balance is maintained; the distillation and filtration processes are vegan-friendly. This version was originally created for an exclusive London club, the Carlton Club, and was so popular that it earnt a place in the small producer's product line. It is an innovative and modern gin, at the same time remaining faithful to the most orthodox London tradition. It is produced in one of the largest distilleries in the city, which operates under the instructions of the producer.

Tasting
Nose: *herbaceous with pine notes.*
Palate: *smooth and savory with very evident balsamic notes.*
Finish: *citric, complex and persistent.*
Ideal: *in Gin & Tonic; rub a slice of lemon around the rim of the glass and then use it to garnish.*

The Gin Daisy

60 ml (2 fl oz) Juniper Green Trophy • 15 ml (1/2 fl oz) pomegranate molasses • 1 lemon

Method: shake&strain • Glass: highball • Garnish: pomegranate seeds and a slice of lemon

For the syrup, mix equal parts water and sugar and boil until the latter has dissolved; add the pomegranate juice and put in the refrigerator.
For the cocktail, put all the ingredients in a shaker with ice and shake. Pour into a highball glass with a few ice cubes and garnish with pomegranate seeds and a slice of lemon.

Martin Miller's 9 Moons

Style: *barrel-aged Dry Gin/contemporary*
Country: *UK-Iceland*
ABV: *40%*
Bottle: *35 cl*
Production: *traditional copper pot still.*

Botanicals: *juniper, coriander, angelica, orange peel, lemon peel, lime oil, iris, cassia, nutmeg, licorice, distilled cucumber.*

Production, which began in 1999, takes place in the Langley distillery, near Birmingham, while the water used to dilute the distillate comes from Iceland; the flags of Iceland and the UK appear side by side on the Martin Miller's label. The recipe for Martin Miller's Gin is based on the use of ten botanicals: the citrus fruits (oranges, lemon and lime peel) are macerated and distilled separately from the rest of the botanicals and then added during the blending stage. The distillery uses a large traditional alembic still, christened Angela by the owners, which is over a century old.

To obtain 9 Moons, the gin is taken to Iceland to age, where there are ideal conditions for slow aging thanks to the dry cold. Here the distillate is aged for "9 moons," i.e. nine months in oak barrels. Each batch is obtained from a single barrel.

Tasting
Nose: *citric and juniper notes with a hint of vanilla and wood.*
Palate: *the citric notes return on the palate with a sweet note of vanilla.*
Finish: *resh and balsamic finish with a spice note of wood.*
Ideal: *neat.*

9 Moons

4 cl (1 1/4 fl oz) Martin Miller's 9 Moons served with 2 ice cubes.

Method: on the rocks • Glass: old fashioned

Pour the gin directly over two large ice cubes in an old fashioned glass.

RADEMON ESTATE

SHORTCROSS

SMALL-BATCH DISTILLERY

GIN

| DISTILLED WITH PRIDE | ALCOHOL | | APPROVED BY DISTILLER |
| *Ireland* | 46% ABV | | *Boyd-Armstrong* |

Shortcross

Style: *Dry Gin/contemporary*
Country: *UK/Northern Ireland*
ABV: *46%*
Bottle: *70 cl*
Production: *Carl 450l copper still with double column.*

Botanicals: *known botanicals include juniper coriander, orange peel, cassia, wild clover, elderflower and elderberry, green apple.*

Shortcross is produced in the Rademon Estate Distillery and particular attention has been paid to the distillery system, produced by the German company Carl, which is composed of traditional 450-liter copper pot still and two enrichment columns, each with seven bubble plates enabling them to set just the right level of reflux. The result is an extremely pure and light distillate. Born in 2012 from the idea of a couple, Fiona and David Boyd-Armstrong, this gin is an ode to Irish green, with the presence of clover, the island's symbol, giving it a herbaceous undertone, and the addition of elder berries and green apple. The product line also includes a barrel-aged gin and a few limited editions.

Tasting

Nose: *delicate with balsamic, fruity and elderflower notes.*
Palate: *full-bodied and embracing, with apple and elderflower notes and a herbaceous undertone with hints of juniper.*
Finish: *long and smooth.*
Ideal: *in Gin & Tonic with elderflower Fever Tree tonic and a mint leaf to garnish.*

9 Hour Bill

*35 ml (1 1/6 fl oz) Shortcross gin • 10 ml (1/3 fl oz) Campari •
20 ml (2/3 fl oz) orange juice • 10 ml (1/3 fl oz) lemon juice •
10 ml (1/3 fl oz) sugar syrup • 15 ml (1/2 fl oz) egg white*

*Method: dry shake, shake&strain • Glass: cocktail
Garnish: orange peel twist*

Put the ingredients in a shaker without ice and shake. Add ice and shake vigorously. Pour into a chilled cocktail glass and serve with an orange peel twist.

SKIN
GIN

HANDCRAFTED
GERMAN
DRY GIN

Skin Gin Gruppe
Alter Marktplatz 6
21720 Steinkirchen
Germany

500 ML | 42% VOL.

Skin Gin

Style: *Dry Gin/contemporary*
Country: *Germany*
ABV: *42%*
Bottle: *70 cl*

Production: *Holstein copper stills.*
Botanicals: *juniper, Vietnamese coriander, Moroccan mint, lime, orange, lemon and grapefruit peel.*

Skin Gin is the brainchild of a Danish businessman, Martin Birk Jensen, and the first gin was produced in 2015. Work started much earlier, with a careful study on the packaging, overseen by designer Mathias Rüsch, which has a unique "skin" that evokes the brand name, covering the bottle to offer a tactile experience. Customers, including private ones, can contact the company and request a customized bottle or have their own version of Skin Gin made. The taste is enhanced by the use of four citrus fruits and by the freshness of mint and coriander. Each botanical is distilled separately in two types of Holstein stills and they are then blended together and diluted to obtain the finished product.

Tasting

Nose: *fresh and citric with strong notes of grapefruit and mint.*
Palate: *a subdued note of juniper leaves space for the citric note of the four different citrus fruits, coriander and the freshness of the mint.*
Finish: *complex, long and fresh.*
Ideal: *in Gin & Tonic with an orange peel twist and garnished with a sprig of rosemary.*

Gin Hot Toddy

40 ml (1 1/4 fl oz) Skin Gin • 25 ml (2/3 fl oz) lemon juice • 60 ml (2 fl oz) hot water • 5 ml (1/6 fl oz) honey

Method: build • Glass: cup • Garnish: cinnamon stick

Put the honey in the cup; add the gin, lemon and hot water and stir until the honey has dissolved. Garnish with a cinnamon stick.

Style: *Dry Gin/contemporary*
Country: *UK/Scotland*
ABV: *46%*
Bottle: *70 cl*
Production: *Lomond copper still.*
Botanicals: *Angelica root, apple Mint, birch leaves, bog myrtle, cassia, chamomile, cinnamon, coriander, creeping thistle,elderflowers,gorse, heather,hawthorn, juniper, lady's bedstraw, lemon. liquorice, meadow sweet, orange peel, oris, peppermint, mugwort, red clover, sweet cicely, tansy, thyme, water mint, white clover, wood sage.*

Botanist is proudly produced at the Bruichladdich Distillery, on the island of Islay, which is famed for its peated whisky.

The distillery uses a Lomond still, previously used for the distillation of whisky at Inverleven, which combines the concepts of a traditional still with those of a distillation column. Its odd shape led Scottish journalist Tom Morton to describe the still as "an oversized upside-down dustbin made of copper," and in the distillery it was baptized with the name of *Ugly Betty*, due to its lack of elegance. The distillation process is very slow; the still is first heated to a temperature that is not sufficient for distillation and some of the botanicals are added, in a precise order, where they are left to steep for about twelve hours. The temperature is then raised and the vapors pass through the other botanicals in the upper part of the still. The number 22, which is clearly visible on the label, indicates the number of botanicals, which include thirteen that are collected on the island, one of which is "bog myrtle," a typical Scottish plant.

Tasting

Nose: *menthol notes of spices, citrus fruits and flowers.*
Palate: *hot and smooth, with a subdued juniper note leaving space for the citrus notes.*
Finish: *fresh with marine and balsamic notes.*
Ideal: *in a Martini with a light Vermouth.*

White Negroni

30 ml (1 fl oz) Botanist Gin • 60 ml (2 fl oz) Cocchi Americano • 15 ml (1/2 fl oz) Luxardo Maraschino • 4 drops of grapefruit bitter

Method: stir&strain • Glass: old fashioned
Garnish: slice of orange peel

Put all of the ingredients in a mixing glass with ice and stir. Pour into an old fashioned glass filled with ice. Garnish with a slice of orange peel.

Ungava

Style: *Local/contemporary*
Country: *Canada*
ABV: *43%*
Bottle: *70 cl*

Production: *maceration of a few botanicals after distillation.*
Botanicals: *juniper and local herbs, including Labrador tea, bearberry, cloudberry and wild rose.*

Ungava takes its name from the bay to the north of Quebec, where a large part of the herbs that give the gin its characteristic yellow color are collected. In addition to juniper, the gin is produced with a mixture of herbs and berries found in the area, including a rhododendron species typical of the Arctic, known by the locals as Labrador tea.
The yellow color is due to the infusion of herbs after distillation and the alcohol is produced using Canadian corn.

Tasting
Nose: *juniper, citrus fruits and a fresh herbaceous note.*
Palate: *sweet and fruity.*
Finish: *fresh and balsamic.*
Ideal: *in a Gibson.*

Signature Pour

60 ml (2 fl oz) Ungava Gin • Half a grapefruit

Method: build • Glass: old fashioned • Garnish: grapefruit twist

Squeeze half a grapefruit into the glass; add large ice cubes and then the gin. Stir and garnish with a grapefruit twist.

Williams
Elegant
Chase

Style: *Gin with distilled organic cider/ contemporary*
Country: *UK*
ABV: *48%*
Bottle: *70 cl*

Production: *Carter-Head 400l copper stills.*
Botanicals: *malt, elderflower, Bramely apples, angelica, juniper and other ingredients.*

The Elegant variation of Gin Chase is one of the cornerstones of the worldwide rebirth of gin and one of the first to focus on the raw base material. The Chase family, an agricultural producer since the early 2000s, mainly of potatoes, tried a more direct connection with their consumers by selling products directly, and in 2008 they decided to set up a distillery. The first product was a potato vodka, which was then used as a base to produce the first gin. The base alcohol used for Elegant is however organic apple cider, produced on the same farm, which passes through a distillation column and emerges with 80% vol. The difference compared to potato alcohol is evident; apple alcohol is more fragrant and full-bodied and has a delicate citric note. An incredible sixteen tons of apples is needed to make a thousand liters of alcohol. The distillate is then mixed with water and alcohol before being re-distilled in a Carter-Head, in which the botanical oils, placed in the basket over the still, are extracted from the distillation vapors. The entire production process takes place within the company, and the gin has the words "Single Estate" on the label. Williams GB is among the other products and there are two editions characterized by citrus fruits (Grapefruit and Seville Orange) with a base alcohol produced from potatoes.

Tasting
Nose: *delicate with evident floral and fruity notes.*
Palate: *smooth, round and fruity with predominant apple and a balsamic note of juniper.*
Finish: *rich, persistent and smooth.*
Ideal: *in Gin & Tonic garnished with a slice of apple.*

The Apple Leaf

40 ml (1 1/4 fl oz) Williams Elegant Chase Gin • 10 ml (1/3 fl oz) elderflower liqueur • 12.5 ml (1/3 fl oz) lemon juice • 10 ml (1/3 fl oz) grenadine syrup • 20 ml (2/3 fl oz) egg white

Method: shake&double strain • Glass: martini • Garnish: mint leaf

Put the ingredients in a shaker with ice and shake vigorously. Sieve twice, the second time into a chilled martini glass. Garnish with a small mint leaf.

Innovative Gins

G'Vine Floraison

Gin Mare

Ginraw

Hendrick's

Malfy

Monkey 47

Santamania Four Pillars

Sipsmith V.J.O.P

There are several approaches that can be used for a gin to hold its own among a growing number of references and brands.

Many new producers have approached the market by doing and conceiving things in a completely different way. Ingredients never used before, complex and extremely well-structured production techniques that also utilize modern equipment, distillery teams with professionals from other sectors, for example, fashion, the perfume industry, as well as from the world of cooking; these are just a few of the paths that producers choose to follow. Hendrick's uses a complex production process and unusual aromas like cucumber, a tribute to the typical British picnic sandwich, and Gin Mare, with its modern Mediterranean edge, has without a doubt been one of the cornerstones of innovation in the sector. In recent years, innovation has gone one step further, and gin has met other disciplines such as cooking, with the introduction of a tool used by chefs, the Rotaval, for example in the production of Ginraw. Innovation also finds its place in the revival and reinvention of ancient gin-making methods: for example, G'Vine, produced in an area with a different vocation, Cognac, uses wine as the base alcohol.

G'Vine Floraison

Style: *Gin distilled with wine/innovative*
Country: *France*
ABV: *40%*
Bottle: *70 cl*

Production: *three types of traditional copper pot stills.*
Botanicals: *juniper, ginger, licorice, cassia, cardamom, coriander, nutmeg, Giava pepper, lime peel, grapevine flowers.*

G'Vine is the brainchild of Jean-Sebastien Robicquet and can be considered a meeting point between the world of wine and the origins of gin produced with wine distillates. G'Vine comes from one of the areas most well-known for grape distillates, the Cognac region. As well as providing fruit to produce the base alcohol, the vines also provide the flowers which are among the botanicals. The flowers are left to macerate in alcohol for several days before being distilled in a small Florence still. The remaining botanicals are also distilled separately in a copper still. The distillates are then mixed together with more wine alcohol and re-distilled in a third still, called "Lily Fleur." The product line also includes G'Vine Nouaison, which, instead of the flowers, is made with the small berries that begin to form after the flowering stage.

Tasting
Nose: *floral and fruity with juniper notes.*
Palate: *dry with balsamic and floral notes.*
Finish: *floral and persistent with lemon notes.*
Ideal: *in Gin & Tonic, garnished with a skewer of white grapes.*

Grape Martinez

45 ml (1 1/2 fl oz) G'Vine Gin Floraison • 30 ml (1 fl oz) red Vermouth •
2 tbsp lemon juice • A handful of red grapes • 2.5 ml (1/12 fl oz) sugar syrup

Method: shake&strain • Glass: Coupette • Garnish: skewer of red grapes

Crush the grapes with a pestle or blend them. Put all of the ingredients in a shaker with ice. Shake for at least a minute and then pour into a chilled Coupette.
Garnish with a skewer of grapes.

Gin
Mare

GIN MARE

DISTILLED FROM OLIVES, THYME, ROSEMARY AND BASIL.

700 ml.   Alc. 42,7 % vol.

Style: *Mediterranean/innovative*
Country: *Spain*
ABV: *42.7%*
Bottle: *70 cl*

Production: *Traditional 250l Florence copper stills.*
Botanicals: *basil, thyme, rosemary, citrus fruits, juniper, coriander, cardamom, Arbequina olives.*

Gin Mare is one of the historical precursors of the new gin of the third millennium. This gin was launched in 2008 by a joint venture consisting of a historical producer of Spanish gin, the Ribot family, and a company specialized in the production of premium brands, and is characterized by the use of Mediterranean botanicals, including olives. The iconic bottle, with a lid that also serves as a measuring cup, was introduced in 2012 and in just a few years has earnt its place behind bars all over the world. For each production process 15 kilos of Arbequina olives are needed and the citrus fruits used are macerated in an aqueous-alcoholic solution, with 50% alcohol, for about a year. The other botanicals are soaked in alcohol for about 36 hours and each one is distilled separately for about four hours in Florence copper stills. The distillates obtained are then mixed together, more neutral alcohol is added and the gin is brought to the final alcohol level. The juniper comes from the Ribot family's crops.

Tasting
Nose: *Mediterranean botanicals with predominant herbaceous notes of thyme and juniper emerging.*
Palate: *balsamic notes of juniper and evident thyme, basil and rosemary notes.*
Finish: *complex and herbaceous with a note of olive and citrus fruits.*
Ideal: *in Gin & Tonic with a sprig of thyme.*

Red Sea

50 ml (1 3/4 fl oz) Gin Mare • 20 ml (2/3 fl oz) vanilla syrup • Juice of one lime • 3 slices of red pepper • 1 spring of thyme

Method: shake&double strain • Glass: old fashoned
Garnish: julienne of dehydrated red pepper

Fill the shaker with three pieces of fresh pepper, the sprig of thyme and the lime juice and shake. Add the rest of the ingredients and ice and shake energetically until you get a smooth liquid. Sieve twice, the second time into an old fashioned glass filled with crushed ice. Garnish with julienne slices of dehydrated red pepper.

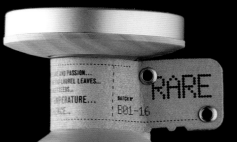

Ginraw

BATCH Nº B01-16

RARE

...and passion...
...no-laurel leaves...
...seeds...
...temperature...
...se...

Crafted **with botanicals distilled**
at low temperature in

BARCELONA

GASTRONOMIC GIN

GINRAW

RARE

BOTTLE Nº: 01455/05000

A CUTTING-EDGE GIN, THE PERFECT BLEND OF TALENT,
MODERNITY AND TRADITION. FINISHED WITH FRESH BOTANICALS
CAREFULLY DISTILLED AT LOW TEMPERATURE, CAPTURES
THE ESSENCE OF BARCELONA'S UNIQUE LIFESTYLE.

Distilled Gin
42.3% VOL
70 CL

Style: *gastronomic/innovative*
Country: *Spain*
ABV: *42.3%*
Bottle: *70 cl*

Production: *traditional copper pot stills and Rotaval.*
Botanicals: *juniper, lemon, cedar, kaffir lime leaves, black cardamom, coriander, bay leaf.*

Ginraw is the brainchild of two marketeers who are incredibly passionate about Barcelona, Roger Burgués and Luis Jauregui, for many years at the forefront of research on foods; one need only think of molecular cuisine. After many years in the drinks industry, the two founders decided to put together a team, made up of Rossend Mateu, maître parfumeur, Sergi Figueras, sommelier, Javier Caballero, mixologist, and Xano Saguer, chef. The aim was to create an extremely innovative product using the various experiences of the team, as well as taking advantage of technology.

The production process is divided into two parts: the juniper-flavored base alcohol is produced with a traditional method in copper stills, but added to this is the product obtained from a Rotaval, a machine that is widely used by great chefs, which permits the extraction of oils at low temperatures, around 25° C. The result is a smooth gin with very distinct and distinguishable aromas, which have maintained all of the properties of the initial botanicals. It is for this reason that Ginraw defines itself as a gourmet gin.

Tasting
Nose: *predominant citric note, spicy.*
Palate: *smooth and all of the ingredients distinguishable from the juniper, with the citrus fruits standing out.*
Finish: *fresh, herbaceous, complex and well-balanced.*
Ideal: *in Gin & Tonic with slices of Granny Smith apple and ginger.*

Rare Sazerak

60 ml (2 fl oz) Ginraw • 1 sugar cube • 2 dash of grapefruit bitter • Aromatizing spray

Method: stir&strain • Glass: Coupette • Garnish: lemon twist

Dissolve the sugar in a mixing glass with ice and the other ingredients; bring to the desired temperature and level of dilution. Pour into a chilled Coupette and aromatize with a spray of your choice (e.g. chamomile, lavender). Complete with a lemon twist and garnish.

Style: *Dry Gin/innovative*
Country: *UK*
ABV: *41.4% (44% for some markets and duty free)*
Bottle: *70 cl*
Production: *Bennett and Carter-Head traditional copper stills.*

Botanicals: *milfoil, coriander, juniper, chamomile, cumin seeds, cubeb berries, elderflower, orange peel, lemon peel, angelica root, orris root. Cucumber essences and Bulgarian Damask rose petals are added at the end of the process.*

In 1966, Charles Gordon, the great-grandson of William Grant, founder of the Glenfiddich and Balvenie distilleries, bought two stills historically used to produce gin, a carter-head and a Bennett at an auction selling off the property of Marshall Taplow, an old distiller active in East London since 1760. In 1999 the two stills at the Girvan distillery begin to produce Hendrick's. The name was chosen by Charles Gordon's mother, who suggested a tribute to gardener, who had lovingly cared for her roses. The production process is complex: the two stills use the same botanicals and the obtained distillates are then mixed together; the ratios are a well-kept secret. The Bennett still produces bolder aromas, in particular those of juniper, lemon and the earthier aromas of the roots; the Carter-Head produces lighter and more floral notes, extracted from the basket by the distillation vapors. After blending, the distillate is brought to the final alcohol level and the cucumber and rose petal essences are added.

Tasting

Nose: *floral, herbaceous and fresh with citrus notes.*
Palate: *smooth with citrus notes, sweet.*
Finish: *long and floral with a characteristic herbaceous note of cucumber.*
Ideal: *in Gin & Tonic with a slice of cucumber.*

Forenoon Fizz

60 ml (2 fl oz) Hendrick's Gin • 15 ml (1/2 fl oz) Cointreau • 30 ml (1 fl oz) lemon juice • 1 tsp orange marmalade • Champagne

Method: shake&strain • Glass: double cocktail • Top-up: champagne
Garnish: toasted sliced white bread

Put the gin, marmalade, lemon and Cointreau in a shaker without ice. Shake until the marmalade has completely dissolved. Add ice and shake vigorously. Pour into a flute and top up with champagne. Garnish with a triangle of toasted sliced white bread.

Malfy

Style: *Dry Gin/innovative*
Country: *Italy*
ABV: *41%*
Bottle: *75 cl*

Production: *steel vacuum stills.*
Botanicals: *juniper, lemon and five more including cassia, coriander and angelica.*

Malfy Gin is produced in Moncalieri, on the outskirts of Turin, in a distillery dating back to 1906, which used to be owned by a large international group. In 1992, while he was the technical director of Seagram, Carlo Vergnano founded Torino Distillati and reconverted the plant for the production of quality liqueurs and distillates. Given the success of the main distillery plant, a second plant was opened to produce brandy and in particular for aging in wood barrels. The lemon, peel and juice are macerated in alcohol together with the other botanicals before being vacuum distilled at low temperatures for about four hours. The temperature, lower than 60°C, means that the oils and aromas remain almost intact in the finished product. Malfy was launched on a large scale in 2016.

Tasting

Nose: *extremely predominant lemon and juniper.*
Palate: *well-balanced between juniper and lemon.*
Finish: *refreshing, aromatic and persistent.*
Ideal: *in a Negroni and a Martini.*

Bee's Knees

*60 ml (2 fl oz) Malfy gin • 30 ml (1 fl oz) lemon juice •
30 ml (1 fl oz) honey syrup*

Method: shake&strain • Glass: coupe • Garnish: lemon twist

To make the honey syrup, just add water to the honey and stir until it has completely dissolved. For the cocktail, put all of the ingredients in a shaker with ice and shake. Pour into a chilled coupe glass and garnish with a lemon twist.

*Monkey
47*

Style: *Dry Gin/innovative*
Country: *Germany*
ABV: *40%*
Bottle: *50 cl*
Production: *Holstein copper pot stills.*
Botanicals: *47 botanicals including six types of pepper, acacia, sweet flag, almonds, angelica, bitter orange, blackberries, cardamom, cassia, chamomile, cinnamon, lemon verbena, cloves, coriander, cranberry, Giava pepper, dog rose, elderflower, ginger, grains of paradise, hawthorn berries, ambrette, Chinese hibiscus, honeysuckle, jasmine, kaffir lime, lavender, lemon, Melissa, citronella, licorice, cranberry, Monarda Didyma, nutmeg, iris, pimento, pomelo, rose hip, sage, wild blackthorn, spruce.*

The number that accompanies the name indicates the number of botanicals used in this gin, which is produced in the Black Forest and thereby called Swartzwald Dry Gin. The distillery is housed in an old mill and was founded by Alexander Stein, together with Master Distiller Christoph Keller. When it was launched, in 2008, it was definitely one of the most innovative products on the market, also thanks to the complexity of the recipe. Its success led to the expansion of the distillery, with a new distillation room housing four copper stills. The process starts with the cranberries being macerated in a molasses distillate for about two weeks; oranges are then added for two days, followed by the still-moist ground Croatian juniper and most of the other botanicals. The remaining botanicals are inserted into the still in a bag and are extracted by the distillation vapors. The obtained distillate is left to rest in terracotta amphorae for three months, resulting in a gin that isn't completely clear. A limited edition version is produced annually, Distiller's Cut, with a different recipe each year.

Tasting

Nose: *lavender, flowers, spices and a citrus note; these give way to smooth spiciness and a floral aroma.*
Palate: *fresh balsamic note of juniper, mint and pine, followed by citrus fruits and flowers.*
Finish: *long, warm and spicy.*
Ideal: *neat or on the rocks.*

47 Monkeys

50 ml (1 3/4 fl oz) Monkey 47 • 30 ml (1 fl oz) fresh lemon juice • 20 ml (2/3 fl oz) red grapefruit syrup • 5 ml (1/6 fl oz) Chartreuse Verte • 3 sage leaves

Method: shake & double strain • Glass: highball • Garnish: kaffir lime or lime leaves

Put the ingredients into a shaker with ice, shake and then sieve into a highball glass with ice. Garnish with kaffir lime or lime leaves.

Style: *Gin distilled with wine/innovative*
Country: *Spain/Australia*
ABV: *40%*
Bottle: *70 cl*

Production: *Carl copper stills.*
Botanicals: *juniper, Cornicabra olives, rosemary, savory, almonds, Australian myrtle, wild Australian tomato, mountain pepper.*

Santamania Fours Pillars is an oceanic voyage, an idea born from the collaboration of two brands, a European one, Santamania, and an Australian one, Four Pillars. The Master Distiller of Four Pillars, Cameron Mackenzie, flew from Melbourne to Madrid with his Australian botanicals, actively participating in the production of this gin. Produced in Spain, in the only urban Iberian distillery, this gin is characterized by its base alcohol of Spanish grapes, distilled by Santamania. Santamania produces small batches of maximum 800 bottles, using two Carl copper stills, called Lola and Vera, combined with a rectification column. The Santamania line includes, among others, London Dry Gin, barrel-aged Gin and two different types of vodka.

Tasting
Nose: *the spicy herbaceous note stands out.*
Palate: *smooth, savory and well-balanced ingredients with a sweet note thanks to the alcohol in the wine.*
Finish: *smooth, long and spicy.*
Ideal: *in Gin & Tonic garnished with a sprig of rosemary.*

Rosemary Gimlet

60 ml (2 fl oz) Santamania Four Pillars dry gin • 25 ml (2/3 fl oz) lime juice • 25 ml (2/3 fl oz) rosemary syrup

Method: shake&stir • Glass: coupe • Garnish: slice of lime

For the rosemary syrup, mix equal parts water and sugar and heat together with the finely chopped rosemary, stirring occasionally. Leave to cool, pour into a container and put in the refrigerator. For the Rosemary Gimlet, put all of the ingredients into a shaker with ice and shake for about 30 seconds. Pour into a chilled coupe glass and garnish with a slice of lime.

SIPSMITH®
independent spirits

SIGNATURE EDITION SERIES

V.J.O.P.

Handcrafted by master distiller:

70cl ℮   57.7%vol

Sipsmith V.J.O.P.

Style: *Navy Strength/innovative*
Country: *UK*
ABV: *57.7%*
Bottle: *70 cl*

Production: *Carl column copper stills.*
Botanicals: *Macedonian juniper and other unspecified botanicals.*

Sipsmith V.J.O.P., aka Very Juniper Over Proof, is the raciest gin offered by this brand, both in terms of alcohol content and the intentional intensity of the note of Macedonian juniper. Sipsmith was the first new distillery to open in London for two centuries. It uses a classic distillation method with copper stills and is open to the public. Master Distiller Jared Brow decided to extract the essential oils from the juniper by using all three techniques: alcoholic maceration, steeping during distillation and vapor extraction, with a container in the upper part of the still through which the alcoholic vapors pass. The product line also includes London Dry, Sloe Gin, Lemon Drizzle, a historical product revisited, and London Cup, a gin infused with Earl Grey tea, with 29.5% vol. There is also a vodka.

Tasting

Nose: *predominant pine notes of juniper, followed by a scent of cedar wood.*
Palate: *sweet with a fresh note of juniper and well-balanced coniferous notes.*
Finish: *smooth and persistent with coriander and licorice notes.*
Ideal: *in a Gimlet.*

Boston Meet Prudence

40 ml (1 1/4 fl oz) Sipsmith V.J.O.P. • 25 ml (2/3 fl oz) Palo Cortado Sherry • 15 ml (1/2 fl oz) sweet red Vermouth • 3 dashes of Fernet Branca

Method: stir&strain • Glass: martini • Garnish: orange twist

Pour the ingredients into a mixing glass and stir. Pour into a chilled martini glass and garnish with an orange twist.

Cocktails

 Aviation

 Gibson

 Bijou

 Gimlet

 Clover Club

 Gin Basil Smash

 Corpse Reviver No. 2

 Gin Crusta

 French 75

 Gin Julep

 Gin & Tonic

 Negroni

 Hanky Panky

 Pegu Club

 Jasmine

 Ramos Gin Fizz

 Last Word

 Red Snapper

 Martini Cocktail

 Tom Collins

Aviation

Ingredients

60 ml (2 fl oz) gin
20 ml (2/3 fl oz) lemon juice
7 ml (1/5 fl oz) Crème de Violette
5 ml (1/6 fl oz) Maraschino liqueur

Method: shake&strain • Glass: Coupette
Garnish: cherry

Preparation

Put the ingredients in a shaker with ice and shake. Pour into a coupe glass and garnish with a cherry. Crème de Violette is not always listed in the ingredients as it disappeared from the market for a long time. You will get a dry cocktail with this recipe; if you prefer something sweeter, add more Crème de Violette or sugar syrup, but be careful with the doses. This is a classic cocktail from *The Savoy Cocktail Book*.

Bijou

Ingredients

30 ml (1 fl oz) gin
30 ml (1 fl oz) Red Vermouth
30 ml (1 fl oz) Chartreuse Verte
1 dash orange bitters

Method: stir&strain • Glass: Martini
Garnish: slice of lemon peel

Preparation

Put the ingredients in a mixing glass with ice and stir. Pour into a chilled martini glass and garnish with a slice of lemon peel. This is a classic cocktail from the 1800s. The name refers to the colors of precious stones: the gin is a diamond, the Vermouth a ruby and the Chartreuse an emerald. In some recipes yellow Chartreuse is used, but according to Imbibe Magazine and researcher David Wondrich, it is only logical that there should be green, the color of emerald. It's best to use a dry and uncomplicated gin.

Clover Club

Ingredients

50 ml (1 3/4 fl oz) gin
20 ml (2/3 fl oz) lemon juice
15 ml (1/2 fl oz) Americano Cocchi or Lillet Blanc
15 ml (1/2 fl oz) raspberry syrup (125 g or 4 1/2 oz raspberries,
100 g or 3 1/2 oz sugar, 100 ml or 3 1/4 fl oz water)
1 egg white

Method: dry shake, shake&strain
Glass: Coupette
Garnish: raspberries

Preparation

Put the ingredients in a shaker without ice and shake. Add ice and shake. Pour into a chilled Coupette and garnish with raspberries. You can also use the reverse shake&strain technique; after shaking, pour the drink into a glass without ice and shake for a few more seconds; then pour into the Coupette.

Corpse Reviver No. 2

Ingredients

*20 ml (2/3 fl oz) gin • 20 ml (2/3 fl oz) Lillet Blanc •
20 ml (2/3 fl oz) lemon juice • 20 ml (2/3 fl oz) Orange Curaçao •
2 dashes Absinthe*

*Method: shake&strain • Glass: Coupette
Garnish: slice of lemon peel*

Preparation

Put the ingredients in a shaker with ice and shake. Pour into a coupe and garnish with a slice of lemon peel. It's best to use a dry gin. This is a classic cocktail from *The Savoy Cocktail Book.*

French 75

Ingredients

40 ml (1 1/4 fl oz) gin • 15 ml (1/2 fl oz) lemon juice •
7.5 ml (1/4 fl oz) sugar syrup (ratio water/sugar 1:1)

Method: shake&strain
Glass: Flute • Top-up:
champagne • Garnish: cherry

Preparation

Put the ingredients in a shaker
with ice and shake. Pour into a
flute and top up with
champagne. Garnish with a
cherry or a slice of lemon peel.
This is a variation of the Tom
Collins using champagne.
It is commonly served in a flute,
but it is also very good served
on ice in a Collins glass.

Gibson

Ingredients

60 ml (2 fl oz) gin
1 barspoon Dry Vermouth

Method: stir&strain • Glass: Martini
Garnish: pickled onions

Preparation

Put the ingredients in a mixing glass with ice
and stir. Pour into a chilled Coupette and garnish
with pickled onions.

Gimlet

Preparation

Put the ingredients in a shaker with ice and shake. Pour into a chilled Coupette and garnish with a slice of lime peel. Several big brands have in their own line of ready-made lime cordial, but this cocktail tastes much better if you prepare it yourself. It can also be made with the stir&strain technique. In Japan it is often shaken with caster sugar.

Ingredients

75 ml (2 1/2 fl oz) gin
20 ml (2/3 fl oz) lime juice
20 ml (2/3 fl oz) lime cordial

Method: shake&strain • Glass: Coupette
Garnish: slice of lime peel

Gin Basil Smash

Ingredients

50 ml (1 3/4 fl oz) gin
25 ml (2/3 fl oz) lemon juice
15 ml (1/2 fl oz) sugar syrup
(ratio water/sugar 1:1)
4 basil leaves

Method: shake&double strain
Glass: Old Fashioned
Garnish: basil leaf

Preparation

Put the basil in a shaker and crush gently; add the other ingredients. Shake and sieve into an old fashioned glass with ice. Garnish with a basil leaf. This cocktail, created by Jörg Meyer at the Lion Bar in Hamburg, has become a modern classic.

Ingredients

60 ml (2 fl oz) gin
20 ml (2/3 fl oz) lemon juice
7.5 ml (1/4 fl oz) Orange Curaçao
5 ml (1/6 fl oz) Maraschino liqueur
5 ml (1/6 fl oz) sugar syrup
(ratio water/sugar 1:1)

Method: shake&strain
Glass: Slim Tulip
Garnish: sugar rim on glass
and a slice of orange peel.

Gin Crusta

Preparation

Put the ingredients in a shaker with ice
and shake. Pour into a sugar-rimmed
tulip glass and garnish with a slice
of orange peel.

Gin Julep

Ingredients

60 ml (2 fl oz) gin
1 sugar cube
5 dashes Angostura bitters
5 mint leaves
soda

Method: build
Glass: Tumbler/small tin
Garnish: Sprig of mint and a
dehydrated orange wheel.
You can also add a straw.

Preparation

Moisten a sugar cube with a few drops of Angostura
bitters and put it in a stainless steel glass; a small tin is
perfect. Add the mint and a dash of soda and dissolve the
sugar cube; add cracked ice, pour in the gin and stir. Add a
little more ice and garnish with a sprig of mint and a
dehydrated orange wheel.

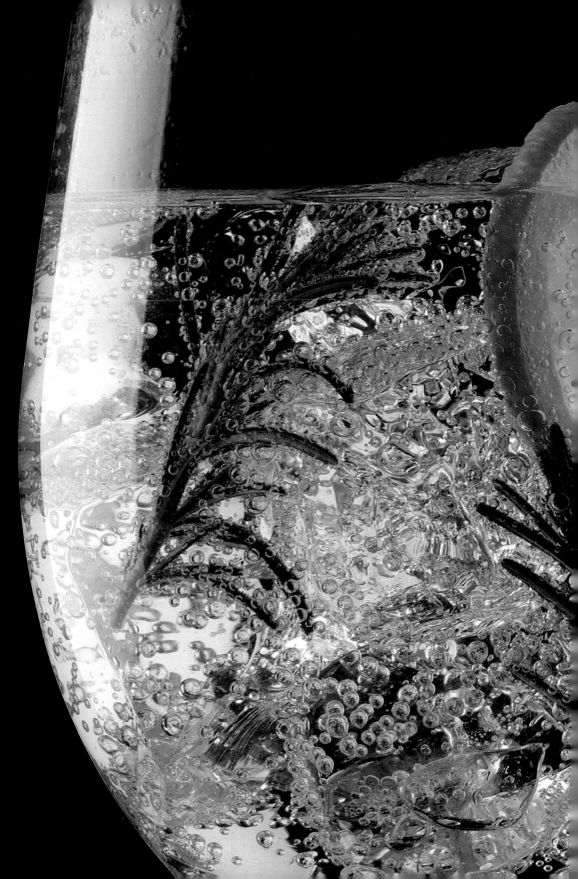

Gin & Tonic

Ingredients

50 ml (1 3/4 fl oz) gin
150 ml (5 fl oz) tonic

Method: build
Glass: Highball or Collins
Garnish: slice of lemon peel

Preparation

Pour the gin and tonic into a large
glass filled with ice, a highball or a
Collins, and stir. You can use a slice
of lemon peel to garnish. Using a
large coupe glass brings out the
aromatic elements of the tonic. The
modern trend is to put a few
botanicals in the glass.

Hanky Panky

Ingredients

50 ml (1 3/4 fl oz) gin
30 ml (1 fl oz) Red Vermouth
5 ml (1/6 fl oz) Fernet Branca

Method: stir&strain
Glass: Coupette
Garnish: slice of orange peel

Preparation

Put the ingredients in a mixing glass with ice and stir. Pour into a chilled Coupette and garnish with a slice of orange peel. A great classic invented by Ada Coleman, bar manager at The Savoy. The name comes from the exclamation actor Charles Hawtrey made after he tasted the drink.
You can also use the throwing method to prepare this cocktail, which involves pouring the ingredients from one vessel to another a few times.

Jasmine

Ingredients

45 ml (1 1/2 fl oz) gin • 20 ml (2/3 fl oz) bitters •
15 ml (1/2 fl oz) lemon • 15 ml (1/2 fl oz) Cointreau

Method: shake&strain • Glass: Coupette
Garnish: slice of lemon peel

Preparation

Put the ingredients in a
shaker with ice and shake.
Pour into a chilled Coupette
and garnish with a slice of
lemon peel. This cocktail
dates back to the mid-1990s
and was created in California;
it is ideal as an aperitif.

Last Word

Ingredients

*20 ml (2/3 fl oz) gin • 20 ml (2/3 fl oz) Chartreuse Verte •
20 ml (2/3 fl oz) Maraschino liqueur • 20 ml (2/3 fl oz) lemon*

*Method: shake&strain • Glass: Coupette
Garnish: dehydrated lime wheel*

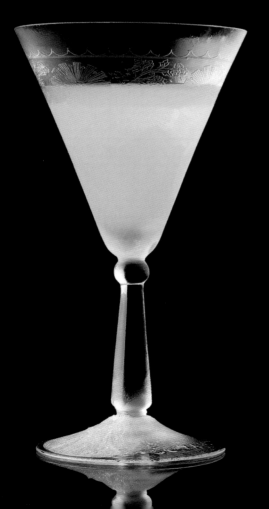

Preparation

Put the ingredients in a
shaker with ice and shake.
Pour into a chilled Coupette
and garnish with a dehydrated
lime wheel. The recipe uses
equal parts of each ingredient.
If you prefer a drier cocktail,
decrease the amount of
Maraschino liqueur. One of
the variations you can try is
using Chartreuse Jaune and
Chartreuse Verte together.

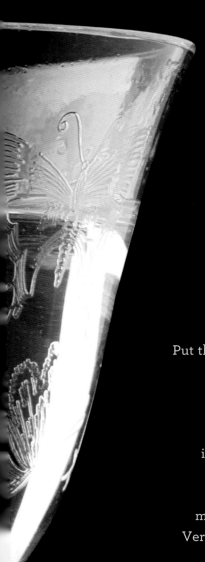

Ingredients

60 ml (2 fl oz) gin
1 barspoon Dry Vermouth
1 dash orange bitters

Method: stir&strain
Glass: Martini
Garnish: olive or lemon to taste

Preparation

Put the ingredients in a mixing glass with ice and stir. Pour into a chilled Coupette and garnish with an olive or slice of lemon peel to taste. The modern trend is to almost completely remove the Vermouth, although initially the Martini was not so markedly dry. The in&out technique is often used with dry Vermouth: pour the Vermouth onto ice in a mixing glass, stir and then pour off the excess Vermouth; then add the other ingredients to the mixing glass.

Martini Cocktail

Negroni

Ingredients

30 ml (1 fl oz) gin
30 ml (1 fl oz) Campari bitter
30 ml (1 fl oz) Red Vermouth
dash of soda

Method: stir&strain
Glass: Old Fashioned
Garnish: slice of orange or slice of lemon peel

Preparation

Put the ingredients in a mixing glass with ice and stir. Pour into an old fashioned glass, directly over ice cubes. Garnish with a slice of orange or a slice of lemon peel. A great classic with many variations; it can also be built and mixed directly in the glass. The stir&strain technique makes it more homogeneous and harmonious. The orange slice can also be considered an ingredient, because it influences the flavor and aroma of the cocktail.

Pegu Club

Ingredients

60 ml (2 fl oz) gin
Half a lime, squeezed
15 ml (1/2 fl oz) Orange Curaçao
2 dashes Angostura bitters
1 dash orange bitters

Method: shake&strain • Glass: Coupette
Garnish: slice of lime peel

Preparation

Put the ingredients in a
shaker with ice and shake
vigorously to assist the oxygenation
of the ingredients. Pour into a chilled
Coupette and garnish with a slice of lime
peel. For lovers of very dry, alcoholic cocktails.

Glass: Collins or Highball
Top-up: 30 ml (1 fl oz) soda
Garnish: a slice of lemon

Preparation

Put all of the ingredients in a
shaker, add ice and shake for
at least two minutes. Pour
into a highball glass and top
up with soda. As it is
necessary to whip the cream
and egg white, you can use a
cappuccino whisk before
adding the ice and shaking.
Garnish with a slice of lemon.

Red Snapper

Ingredients

60 ml (2 fl oz) gin • 90 ml (3 fl oz) tomato juice • 15 ml (1/2 fl oz) lemon • 3-5 juniper berries • 4 dashes Worcestershire sauce • 2 dashes tabasco • 2-3 grinds of black pepper

Method: slow build
Glass: highball or Collins
Garnish: salt rim, first passing the lemon

Preparation

Salt rim the glass, crush the juniper berries and put all of the ingredients directly into the serving glass. Fill with ice and stir until you get the desired consistency. You can also use the throwing method to prepare this cocktail, which involves pouring the ingredients from one vessel to another a few times.

Tom Collins

Ingredients

50 ml (1 3/4 fl oz) gin
30 ml (1 fl oz) lemon juice
15 ml (1/2 fl oz) sugar syrup
(ratio water/sugar 1:1)

Method: shake&strain
Glass: Collins
Top-up: soda
Garnish: slice of lemon peel

Preparation

Put the ingredients in a shaker with ice and shake. Pour into a
Collins glass, top up with soda and garnish with a slice of lemon
peel. Tom Collins is a traditional American cocktail originally
made with Old Tom gin using a shaker and caster sugar. It can
also be made by mixing the ingredients directly in a Collins
glass with ice and soda to taste.

Authors

Davide Terziotti is a great expert in, and lover of, whisky and spirits in general, and since 2009 he has edited the blog "Angel's Share". In 2014, he co-founded the WhiskyClub, whose objective is to spread the knowledge and culture of high-quality spirits by events, courses, festivals, and publishing activities.

Vittorio D'Alberto is the founder of "Gin Italy", a blog born in 2013 and entirely dedicated to gin. The blog is also active on Facebook, Instagram and Twitter. Gin Italy's aim is to highlight the presence of Italian products in the international industry of gin, products that are often underestimated, but essential: just to mention one, the berries of Italian Juniper, shipped from centuries to the United Kingdom. Vittorio D'Alberto is a big fan of Ireland, in his many trips he was intrigued by British spirits, ending up studying and investigating gin in particular.

Fabio Petroni studied photography and then collaborated with the most talented professionals in the industry. His line of work led him to specialize in portraits and still life, areas in which he has shown an intuitive and rigorous style. Working with major advertising agencies, he has participated in numerous campaigns for prestigious companies known worldwide, including major Italian brands.

Ekaterina Logvinova was born in Samara (Russia) in 1988. She graduated in the University of Aerospace Technologies in Economics and Management in Samara and then she moved to Italy, where she graduated in Organization and Human Resources in the State University of Milan. Then she passed in the industry of cocktails, mixology and spirits, her true passion. She worked in Milan bars such as Mag, Julep's, and Terrazza 12 in The Brian&Barry Building and she worked also as a bar manager at The Botanical Club of Milano. Since 2013, she has been working for Elephant Gin as a Brand Ambassador.

Photo credits

Some of the conversions (oz/ml) used in this book must be considered approximations, as the standard measurements used internationally by professional bartenders are always expressed in ounces. The author has chosen to list the doses in milliliters in addition to ounces to facilitate ordinary readers who are amateur bartenders.

Acknowledgement

Thanks also to the The Botanical Club of Milano for their hospitality and help with the photographs of the cocktails.

Our thanks to the following companies:
Beneforti's, Beija Flor, Celebrity, Compagnia dei Caraibi, Diageo Italia, Fine Spirits, Malfy, Mediland, Meregalli, Onesti Group, Primalux Spirits, Shortcross Gin, Skin Gin, Spirits of Indipendence, Velier,

and their representatives:
Paola Algeri, Mathilde de Ramel, Marina del Puppo, Maurizio Andriano, Enrico Magnani, Andrea Gasparri, Maurizio Cagnolati, Roberto D'Alessandro, Jacques Zwartjes, Marco Callegari, Angelo Canessa, Sharon McHarrie, Antonio Beneforti, Massimo Tam, Elwyn Gladstone, Jan Hellwage, Fiona Boyd, Fabio Torretta,

who made this work easier.

A special thanks to the following people for their support and copy editing:

Daniela Daniele, Pietro Fontana, Thais Siciliano, Paolo Tagliabue.

Useful Websites

Beefeater Burrough's Reserve: www.beefeatergin.com

Bluecoat Barrel Reserve: www.bluecoatgin.com

Bulldog: www.bulldoggin.com

Burleigh's Distiller's Cut: www.burleighsgin.com

Caorunn: www.caorunngin.com

Cotswolds: www.cotswoldsdistillery.com

Elephant Gin: www.elephant-gin.com

G'Vine Florasison: www.g-vine.com

Gin Mare: www.ginmare.com

Ginraw: www.ginraw.com

Hayman's Old Tom: www.haymansgin.com

Hendrick's: www.hendricksgin.com

Hernö Juniper Cask Gin: www.hernogin.com

Jensen's Old Tom: www.bermondseygin.com

Juniper Green Trophy Organic: www.junipergreen.org

Malfy: www.malfygin.com

Martin Miller's 9 Moons: www.martinmillersgin.com

Mayfair: www.mayfairbrands.com

Monkey 47: www.monkey47.com

No. 209: www.distillery209.com

Plymouth Navy Strength: www.plymouthgin.com

Santamania Four Pillars: www.santamania.com

Shortcross: www.shortcross.com

Sipsmith V.J.O.P.: www.sipsmith.com

Skin Gin: www.skin-gin.com

Star Of Bombay: www.bombaysapphire.com

Tanqueray Bloomsbury Edition: www.tanqueray.com

Tarquin's: www.southwesterndistillery.com

The Botanist: www.thebotanist.com

Ungava: www.ungava-gin.com

Vallombrosa Gin Dry: www.evallombrosa.it

William Elegant Chase: www.chasedistillery.co.uk

Project editor
VALERIA MANFERTO DE FABIANIS
LAURA ACCOMAZZO

Graphic design
MARIA CUCCHI

WS White Star Publishers® is a registered trademark
property of White Star s.r.l.

© 2017 White Star s.r.l.
Piazzale Luigi Cadorna, 6 - 20123 Milan, Italy
www.whitestar.it

Translation and Editing: TperTradurre s.r.l.

ISBN 978-88-544-1094-7
1 2 3 4 5 6   21 20 19 18 17

Printed in China